THE CONVERSATION
A DANGEROUS DEVICE
RESNIK

PHILOSOPHOETIC

But only for itself is the human a heavy burden! This is because it carries on its shoulders too much that is alien.

F. Nietzche|Thus Spoke Zarathustra

To My Helpmate;
who continues to show me the value of evolved,
loving, fearlessly open and truth-full [conversation].

CALL LOG

CONNECTION ESTABLISHED

It was readily apparent to everyone involved that that vehicle had what they call "dominant battle-space awareness".

C. Mellon|The Phenomenon

This may seem strange at first glance, but a search through the history of how think tanks and other government contractors approached the problem of the UFO phenomenon reveals that they understood (almost from the outset) that this was a problem essentially related to consciousness.

Sekret Machines, Gods|DeLonge, Levenda

According to the rumour...They are beings who are carrying out a cautious survey of the earth and considerably avoid all encounters with men...

C. Jung|Flying Saucers

In many close encounters and abduction reports witnesses are exposed to contact with a form of consciousness that modern science simply does not yet understand.

J. Vallee|Revelations

I'VE BEEN REMINDED RECENTLY, and repeatedly, that we, *The Species we masturbat-orally label, "The Man"*, take this other concept called *"Life"*, entirely, wholly, *too seriously.*

In fact, *The Man*, itself a concept, continues to take all of his sundry concepts much more seriously than himself, and remains quite the paradox that modern Man harbors more acceptance for, and places more power in, *his concept of the Alien, than his own cosmically-evolved self.*

It could be said that the biggest plague of modern Man remains his disease of, *the ease*, with which he so effortlessly and unconsciously continues to hand his own sovereignty, his self-agency, *the right of authority over his own self*, to external agents in the guise of *both Alien and Government.*

> *It's possible that we have been projecting our own image onto the Phenomenon since time immemorial. That may be the key to understanding it.*
>
> Sekret Machines, Man|DeLonge, Levenda

We yet fail, daily, to recognize the long march we have *already successfully made,* out of the dark swamp of mere *passive, animal-awareness,* up, onto dry-land, where we now mold and shape the Earth in *our own image*; one should be weary of their own definition of "image".

Creating in our likeness, and yet, the majority of us still lack *that* next requisite step of growth, *in consciousness*; *awareness*, which enables one *to see the truth* in *why* he paints, *why* he writes, *why* he imagines anything at all.

Reminded indeed that, as long as Man continues to take his *concept of Life* so seriously, *like an animal fearful of a predator in the shadow*, he shall fail to grasp the hilarious simplicity that, *he is not what he believes himself to be.* For the *concept* of *"The Man"*, much like the concept of *"The UFO"*, ...is *lacking.*

It must become apparent that what fails Mankind today is, *his lack of imagination.*

The majority today struggle to out-think their own grandparents, continuing to imagine the dreaded *Alien visitors* and *trans-dimensional beings*, failing to see that these ideas are *themselves very ancient. Ancient Imaginings; Ancient Concepts.*

The modern *Disclosure Disciple* imagines himself at the cusp of *something grand,* not yet accepting that *this something grand, has already happened.* That, he simply remains *the fruit of that something grand.* For our Ancients who *devised* these very concepts, were themselves *The Happening* which, *necessarily leads to the Modern Man.*

Indeed, our very unwillingness to play new games with our brothers and sisters of this playground we call a planet, prevents us from conceptualizing a *new* reality which at once encompasses *each and all of our many varied discoveries* of our own magical selves, both individually and collectively. We must see now that, *the concept of The Man is itself now ancient, and must, like all else in this grand cosmos, evolve. For, when we evolve the concept of The Man, we indeed evolve the very reality he awakes to find himself embedded.*

A cosmically-evolved, biologically-intelligent machine [*The Animal*: The Manimal: The Manchine], now proverbially *"awakening"* to realize *his own truth*: that he is but a small part of a much greater cosmic system.

That The Man is a biological-machine in a garden, approaching and *passing* the ancient *Tree of Knowledge of Good and Evil,* and increasing haste toward, and *aggressively plucking, that forbidden fruit* of the *Tree of Life* itself; accepting his own freedom to now create and manifest his own divine story, within the fated system he finds his sentient self immersed; *using this fated system to his own infinite advantage,* in-fact *hacking The Cosmos* which has birthed him, that he might move his own energetic awareness, *the etherealectricity that he is, within and throughout this cosmically-connected system of cosmos.*

I find it beyond appropriate to begin here, with important words from the founder of analytical psychology, Carl Jung, from his *Flying Saucers, A Modern Myth of Things Seen in the Skies*:

> *"I refer to those reports reaching us from all corners of the earth, rumours of round objects that flash through the tro-posphere and stratosphere, and go by the name of Flying Saucers, soucoupes, disks, and 'Ufos' (Unidentified Flying Objects). These rumours, or the possible physical existence of such objects, seem to me so significant that I feel myself compelled, as once before when events were brewing of fateful consequence for Europe, to sound a note of warning.*

I know that, just as before, my voice is much too weak to reach the ear of the multitude. It is not presumption that drives me, but my conscience as a psychiatrist that bids me fulfil my duty and prepare those few who will hear me for coming events which are in accord with the end of an era.

As we know from ancient Egyptian history, they are symptoms of psychic changes that always appear at the end of one Platonic month and at the beginning of another. They are, it seems, changes in the constellation of psychic dominants, of the archetypes, or 'gods' as they used to be called, which bring about, or accompany, long-lasting transformations of the collective psyche.

This transformation started within the historical tradition and left traces behind it, first in the transition from the age of Taurus to that of Aries, and then from Aries to Pisces, whose beginning coincides with the rise of Christianity. We are now nearing that great change which may be expected when the spring-point enters Aquarius.

It would be frivolous of me to conceal from the reader that reflections such as these are not only exceedingly unpopular but come perilously close to those turbid fantasies which becloud the minds of world-improvers and other interpreters of 'signs and portents'. But I must take this risk, even if it means putting my hard-won reputation for truthfulness, trust-worthiness, and scientific judgment in jeopardy.

I can assure my readers that I do not do this with a light heart. I am, to be quite frank, concerned for all those who are caught unprepared by the events in question and disconcerted by their incomprehensible nature. Since, so far as I know, no one has yet felt moved to examine and set forth the possible psychic consequences of this foreseeable change, I deem it my duty to do what I can in this respect. I undertake this thankless task in the expectation that my chisel will make no impression on the hard stone it meets."

***

THE COMMON MAN CONTINUES to wonder *what it is, truly, that Government knows?*

...there was a commotion in the firmament, and the smallest of all the stars in the Milky Way screamed out: "Now, Peter!"
J.M. Barrie|Peter Pan

Here is where I will only briefly mention another ancient concept in need of evolution: *Astrology*. Do not check-out of our conversation. Do not fear *astrology*. I myself am no astrologer nor prophet of the planets. It makes little sense, admittedly, to a modern man unaware of his own origins, and the part this ancient astrological concept has played in his own psychological development.

Modern Man should consider his modern concepts of computer-programming, and psychology, when considering the ancient concept of *Astrology*.

Now, what does government know? For one thing, *they damn well know Astrology; or, Ustrology, [as I prefer]*. Understand that our *ancient concept* of *Astrology* shall fail us, *today*. We must evolve this concept, to accommodate the modern reality we now stand and awaken to find ourself in the midst of.

Realize that *Astrology does not fail us, we, fail Astrology, by limiting it*.

Our collective lack of imagination fails us all, and is precisely the *reason* we can point our apelike digits at, for why eras end and new ones begin.

It is our ancient concept of Astrology, that must now evolve to become Ustrology. You cannot grasp *Astrology*, necessarily until you grasp your self. Paradoxically, of course, *Ustrology* is perhaps the greatest tool, the greatest concept, we have at our disposal to seek and grasp what a Self might be, and more importantly what he may *not* be.

*NASA named its two-person space capsule Project Gemini after the
zodiac sign because the spacecraft could carry two astronauts.*
Gemini|Wikipedia

Jumping ahead, we can *today*, demand from our own selves: *"No more
delusions of what might be, but simply acceptance of what is."* And *what is, is
Man; the Man; Mankind.* For it has always been *The Man at the center of The
Mandala*; this imaginary universe we reside.

Imaginary, in that Man is not what we think we are; what we were told we
are *supposed-to-be.* It shall take a bold re-write of *the story of The Man,* to see
truth of *both Consciousness and The UFO. We must evolve our concepts,* that we
may evolve this reality that has never quite made...sense. For the very concepts
of "physical", "material", "profane", *must themselves evolve,* for Man to see the
reality behind all these stillborn ideas.

Behind all conceptualized *profane,* there is *awareness of* profane, bundled
together, one-and-in-the-same, for it is merely the sublime mind of the Manimal which necessarily separates and divides, *that it might conquer it's own
nature,* not nature itself. Nature divides not, for this cosmos is the *One united
and quantum-entangled system The Man awakes within, which harbors the
"saving-grace" for his ideas of Immortality of the Self.*

*We know enough, now, to know...*it's not what we hoped it was, and *is* absolutely *what we continue to fear it is. Just...us.*

The obvious connection between our current *concept of Consciousness* and
our current *concept of The UFO,* necessarily begs we begin anew from the
beginning, ensuring these two concepts remain joined as the One they actually
are.

"What beginning?", I hear you ask.

The beginning of what we call, The Man, of course. For *Man remains the one
central and common denominator in all hauntings and happenings, from time
immemorial.*

We must accept that we remain incapable of grasping the *ever-so-out-of-reach
UFO,* not because of its supposed speed, but because of *our slow-growth to
embrace this concept for what it truly is.* That, if Man begins his ascent out of
the cave and savanna with an *immature concept, a malnourished idea, of his very*

own damned self, of who and what and why and where he is, each proceeding generation necessarily begins its own ascent within *a childishly built shack of magic, founded upon a precariously constructed concept.*

Indeed, a vast illusion which continues to increase in both its complexity and simplicity...for it is *the ability of illusory play and imaginings that is the evolved Reality of Mankind,* if, those fearless of us choose to embrace this potential of our own selves.

Surely, *the desire and need for* the ancient concept of *Alien Visitor,* flies out the same mind it arrived from, at the very moment each Man awakens to his very own paradoxically divine evolution; his own self. *The issue is not that the UFO defies reality, the issue is that The Man yet lacks a true grasp of that which he preaches: Reality itself.*

The Man is itself but a malnourished concept, capable of evolution and growth...just as his beloved *Consciousness; Awareness...which,* he is.

Awareness, now aware...*of what?*

Itself, of course.

Awareness aware of itself as such.

Man is *The Awareness, of Mind & Body come-together, joined as one,* now aware of itself, as a necessary subsequent outcome of awareness of Body and Mind grasping eachother under an ancient banner, the ancient concept which he himself actually is: *The Trinity.*

Body, aware of Mind. *Mind,* aware of Body. Joined as one in *"holy matrimony"* to create a cosmic hybrid, *The Man,* a creature whom *moves both in the stars with the gods, as well as on the earth with the animal,* capable of defying both, for *The Man* is *The Child* of these Ancients.

Body and Mind have *always* sought control of The Divine Child we *each* are; control of, *The Awareness.* For as all divorced parents know, *he who controls The Child, controls The Kingdom...*yet the wise child grows to learn that he may manipulate *both Mommy and Daddy, bending both to his will, and each-others,* often bridging a very deep divide.

> *Three hundred years ago a no-man's-land was created between the halves of the bicameral brain, a line drawn along the corpus callosum...The Phenomenon exists there. In that spot.*
> Sekret Machines, Man|DeLonge, Levenda

To truly get at the truth of *Consciousness* and *The UFO*, it benefits us to allow yourself to imagine that *Man* is not quite what perhaps he was told he was. That, perhaps *Man, is* that, and yet *at once so very much more.* If *The Man* wants to grab-hold *The UFO,* he must get out of the way of himself. It should strike you that the infamous Nietzsche, as have many thousands of others, expressed the same sentiment of overcoming yourself, that something *Super* might then you become.

It should be easy to grasp now that, you grasp not *The UFO* necessarily because *you grasp not your own self.* You grasp not, the implications of a lacking, tired, *ancient concept of the Man himself; yourself.* You are, not, what you have ignorantly imagined yourself to be.

All evolves, especially and including, *our ideas.*

All old things must evolve or be relegated to the cosmic-dustbin, for possible re-purposing at some potential future moment if needed, and this includes one of the most ancient, and thus *most in need of evolving* concepts we have in our bag of words, and that is, "*Man*".

We tic our boxes and cross our *T's* in scientific exploration and examination and critique of all "*The Other*", failing always to examine and critique humbly and sincerely, and in fact boldly, *our own damned Selves.* We increase exponentially our reach and knowledge of all external, not realizing the concept of "*The Man*" himself has fallen dangerously behind.

The very *idea of us, of who and what we are and why we do what we do*, is precariously close to that "*cosmic dustbin*".

We must evolve ourselves, both in body and mind, harmoniously, that the true human may himself grow exponentially more liberated; for *the true Man is, The Awareness* created by the balanced joining of *body and mind become aware of each-other,* forming *The Hybrid Being* that we each are, *capable of traversing both spirit and material "realms", necessarily because The Man is not either one of those, but the awareness of both at once.*

The Man is *The Bridge* that *spans the gap between mind and body, the necessary rainbow that joins the spermatozoa known as the Left-Hemisphere, with the egg that remains the Right-Hemisphere.* Hardware and Software working together now, to create *The Experience that is, Awareness of each.*

Masculine and Feminine, Paternal with Maternal, Romeo and Juliet, Beauty and Beast, defying all odds to *birth a New King to this now united Kingdom.*

Ultimately, none of what has been said, or what is to follow, necessarily precludes the very obvious reality that there are surely other intelligent states of existence *"out there"*, *waaayyyy "out there"*.

What all of this *is* to say, *is this*: That we shall never be able to accurately *"see"* these others, *until we are united and joined as a species, that we no longer deceive each-other, yet more importantly yourself.* That, *Man, right now and heretofore, is and has always been absolutely enough to answer all of our questions about Life and Cosmos, and any projection of authority onto an Alien or Government outside of our own self-being, shall only deter us longer from the simple truth and reality that has always been right before us; truth that — We are Man, and, We are enough.*

We are not alone, necessarily because, *we have each-other;* and, we deny this at our own peril.

The truly discerning and wise can see, that, the very moment Mankind *unites as One species,* truly in harmony *for the greater good of The Whole without sacrificing the sovereignty of the Individual,* is the exact moment we make contact with our *actual Cosmic Siblings.* The wise know, *The Cosmos that we surely are, loves naught more than, Balance.* We shall never see an *actual "other",* until we can actually see *ourselves within each-other.*

I sabbath here, Seeker, acknowledging how I began this conversation with you, with the thought that, *we may be taking this all a bit too seriously.*

I accept that the many pages here are enough for us to begin our journey together into the ever-brightening future we now share...with as much love as you can accept, I wish you and your family well and await your response to this, an ongoing communique between the newest of cosmic communicators.

> *It is difficult, if not impossible, to form any correct idea of these objects, because they behave not like bodies but like weightless thoughts.*
>
> C. Jung|Flying Saucers

The Conversation, begins here; now hear!
I accept that the difficult work, the grueling work, has been accomplished.

The forces that pull our disk are "illusory" only to the man who decides to use their energy to run an engine. Perceptually and artistically, they are quite real.

R. Arnheim|Art and Visual Perception

All these words, I don't just say
And nothing else matters
Trust I seek and I find in you
Every day for us something new
Open mind for a different view
And nothing else matters

Metallica|Nothing Else Matters

1

THE GRID

SEEKER, LET US HAVE a conversation together about your hopes and fears surrounding the concepts of, the proverbial *Alien* and his *UFO*. [It could potentially resemble something like the following.]:

***

GREETINGS, [*INSERT YOUR NAME here.*]
  I think you'll appreciate this song: "*The Grid*" by Daft Punk. Give it a listen.
  —*Resnik*

***

[*AND THEN YOU RESPOND.*]
  Resnik,
  Awesome track. I've got a lot of wild ideas myself, about consciousness, and those damn aliens. Ideas that are unique to me but, not truly. I intuit this to be so, yet fear accepting my lack of originality in these matters that seem to concern me so tirelessly. Sharing my thoughts would do wonders for alleviating this pressure I feel building inside.
  Oh, I also pretty much have a *mystical* sort of *belief* in *Extra Sensory Perception*, but suffer under the inability to reconcile this faith with my pre-programmed, western, scientifically analytical mindset.
  I'll send a file to you with some thoughts that *I can't get out of my head.* Good luck!
  —[*Insert your name here.*]

***

Seeker,

Extremely interested in your ideas. (*A bit bored with ancient texts at the moment, as they repeatedly say the same thing, over and over, so I'm looking for new modern concepts from peers*).

If it's acceptable, I'll review your notes and make a few of my own to send back. I firmly accept the old thought of "*where two or more are gathered*" of the Christians. *We are powerful indeed when united.* Send your wild thoughts to:
solunarukh@protonmail.com
—*Resnik*

***

Resnik,

File sent. *Welcome to my mind.* It's a bit of a mess but, there's a method to the madness...I think. Let me know your thoughts.
—[*Insert your name here.*]
Attachment: *Crazy ShiZ.docx*

***

Seeker,

Quite the interestingly shitty read. I'll give it all some thought and respond appropriately to your massive pile of crazy.
—*Resnik*

2
AS AWAKE, SO ASLEEP

Mrs. Darling did not know what to think, for it all seemed so natural to Wendy that you could not dismiss it by saying she had been dreaming.

J.M. Barrie|Peter Pan

The study of consciousness is foundational to the study of the Phenomenon...

DeLonge, Levenda|Sekret Machines, Man

Dream lofty dreams, and as you dream, so shall you become. Your vision is the promise of what you shall one day be; your Ideal is the prophecy of what you shall at last unveil. The greatest achievement was at first and for a time a dream. The oak sleeps in the acorn; the bird waits in the egg; and in the highest vision of the soul a waking angel stirs. Dreams are the seedlings of realities.

J. Allen|As A Man Thinketh

Hence I say we must begin by recognizing the great reach of intellectual territory which is covered by what are called concepts.

G.J. Romanes|Mental Evolution in Man

For Jung and Maeder, this alteration of the conception of the dream brought with it an alteration of all other phenomena associated with the unconscious.

S. Shamdasani|The Red Book

SEEKER,

If we evolve the concept of our own selves, that we now accept the very idea of *"The Man"* to be: *The evolved Being, [or "Thing"], of Awareness, whose essence and nature is centrally and necessarily "ethereal", an "Awareness-Thing", created by the joining together of, awareness of body and awareness of mind, forming a hybrid awareness of both-come-together as One, known universally now as a Higher-Awareness, or "Self".* In short, a *harmonizing of Right Hemisphere and Left Hemisphere,* for the greater good of the whole organism, *The Trinity of Body, Mind, Soul* [Soul=*The Awareness,* that *The Man, actually is*];

We then accept easily that the animal body and mind are necessarily programmed, rhythmically, and a significant part of the programming is to ensure rest for the animal machine during times of what we conceptualize and call *"sleep",* yet *The Man* being not the Body, or the Mind, but a *Being Of Awareness* of both of these, *remains the same, his own Self, regardless of the Body and Mind being in a state of alert "wakefulness" or restful "sleepiness", and that Self is, simply, Awareness.*

We need to take a good, long look at ourselves and the way our minds work.

DeLonge, Levenda|Sekret Machines, Man

Thus, *the concept of dreaming,* itself subsequently evolves, from a *passive* event of an animal body and mind, to *an active participatory experience of The Awareness, [the True Man, if he accepts himself as such].* Therefore, *what Man is while "awake", is exactly what he remains to be while the mind and body of the animal-machine both "sleep".*

Man may embrace this potential, and harness *the infinite abyss that is cosmic-awareness,* to free himself to imagine and create, *while* his gravity-bound body rests. The idea of sleep then becomes more aligned with a sort of meditation; a contemplation.

We can evolve our own Self, as well as *the concept* of *Sleep*, to where, now, rather than laying down each night to passively sleep like an animal, we, the true you as a creature of Awareness, actively rise and awaken to the potential of *a night of uninterrupted contemplation, creation, planning, writing, connecting, etc... That the morning brings naught but gifts of gold to the fearless nighttime journeyman.*

> *...but in the two minutes before you go to sleep it becomes very nearly real. That is why there are night-lights.*
>
> J.M. Barrie|Peter Pan

I pause, to contemplate the proverbial ancient wisdom, to *"know thyself"*, in that this is the path toward knowing, *The All*. Thus, when I take a moment to determine information that may *not* be associated with my Self, I quickly see revealed...*absolutely nothing*; that, *the Self is necessarily and always connected to all else, and it is this knowledge we seek to confirm in this modern epoch of Man.*

We have always, from the proverbial Dawn, intuited our connection to both *"higher"* and *"lower"* supposed-imaginary realms, as conceptualized, visualized, by our yet beloved and worshiped, Ancients. Flipping this then, quickly, we see that when we attempt to determine information, *affirmatively* associated with the Self, we gain access to *all; everything.*

Accepting, or *even temporarily and hesitatingly assuming, your own inherent connection to The All*, regardless of our still ignorant grasp of this possibility, instantly enables access to previously darkened corners of our collective-awareness. It is the acknowledgment and acceptance of the Self *as but part of a greater-whole, a bigger "system", that enables "Neo" to awake from his blue-pilled dream, gaining access to a much wider reality that had been right before his eyes from the beginning.*

There *is* a proverbial *Matrix* of what we conceptualize as data, a "grid-of-information" that, is our very actual *foundation*, as *Beings, Of, Awareness.*

What many and most today have neither time nor stomach for, thus refuse to accept, is that we may indeed have to *go back to this very foundation, The Origin*, of what we consider *The Man "to-be or not-to-be"*, fearless of what

new, wider, more evolved truth may be revealed. Indeed, perhaps we ran before we could comfortably stand, with these giant heads of ours. Telling ourselves a half-conceived story of *what* and *who* we are as evolved creatures of this ...thing... we have conceptualized and labeled for ourselves to be Cosmos.
   —*Resnik*

It is needful for the enamored soul, in order to attain to its desired end, to do likewise, going forth at night, when all the domestics in its house are sleeping and at rest —that is, when the low operations, passions and desires of the soul (who are the people of the household) are, because it is night, sleeping and at rest.
St. John of the Cross|The Dark Night Of The Soul

Grasp: you may lay down your body and not your, Self. That, while animals innocently dream, gods plan, devise, seek, initiate, conspire, and live, ...in the infinite black of the Abyss.
The Philosophoet|Philosophoetic

Dream until the dream come true

Aerosmith|Dream On

"Wendy, Wendy, when you are sleeping in your silly bed you might be flying about with me saying funny things to the stars."
J.M. Barrie|Peter Pan

It was only his imagination that was fed by these initiatory scenarios; but the life of the imagination, like the life of a dream, is as important for the whole psyche of the human being as is daily life.
M. Eliade|Rites and Symbols of Initiation

3

THE YOU.F.O.

Seeker,

As long as there remain *men-of-deception, secret clubs, warfare, capital-ism, and black-budget projects,* Man today cannot *seriously* consider *The UFO* as relating to *actual,* traditionally conceived, *"space visitors"* or *"oth-er-dimensional travelers".*

Man must first get out of his own way, to perceive truth.

We know too much, now, about *Psyche, ESP,* and *Deception,* to consider anything else other than, *the truth of Man himself,* and his incessant chas-ing of his own tale.

A large issue today is, words and language, thus *concepts.*

We so easily get caught-up in our words and ideas; innocently so, thus, we must be ever more *vigilant* when we begin to have greater awareness of these, our patterns and programming.

"The UFO is sending us messages though, right?! What's that all about?", you've asked of me repeatedly.

The UFO is, simply, without separation or distinction between two supposed-to-be disparate concepts [*UFO and Consciousness*], a symbolic attempted visualization [*consciousization*] within awareness, *of Awareness, The Awareness,* that we in fact *are,* thus *we are The UFO. We, are the information projected, and "It" is Us.*

"What the fuck, Resnik?! I don't even know what that is supposed to mean. You've surely lost your way." you quickly snap at me, interrupting truth in full flow and flex.

Remember that the *Self, necessarily also a concept,* is at all times connected to this informational *"matrix of information"* we like to call the "unconscious". We can work on the details of how this is made possible, but *much is gained initially by simply accepting that this is in fact truth [our ultimate connection to each-other and all else, "The Cosmos"].*

> *The soul was supposed to have the form of a sphere, on the analogy of Plato's world-soul, and we meet the same symbol in modern dreams. This symbol, by reason of its antiquity, leads us to the heavenly spheres, to Plato's "super-celestial place" where the "Ideas" of all things are stored up. Hence there would be nothing against the naive interpretation of UFOs as "souls".*
>
> *...I have defined this spontaneous image as a symbolical representation of the self, by which I mean not the ego but the totality composed of the conscious and the unconscious. I am not alone in this, as the Hermetic philosophy of the Middle Ages had already arrived at very similar conclusions.*
>
> C. Jung|Flying Saucers

There is no *belief, no faith required here:* only a humbled, sincere—simple acceptance of an evolved idea of *The Man itself. You.*

Any who humbly and sincerely seek to determine their own connection to this Cosmos *that we are,* shall be greatly and *rapidly* rewarded with such things as, *images and thoughts, full of information.*

Jung clearly and effortlessly stated his own concept of *The UFO,* as a symbolical, archetypal *projection from your Unconscious Reality [that which is "dark" to you, yet not necessarily to all others], upon and into the fragile and lacking Conscious Reality.* A projection of *"wholeness",* indicating a vital step of growth and psychological "healing" [read: balance] within the "patient" that Jung called *"individuation".*

We can fast forward a bit to today, and see how re-conceptualizing *"The Man"* as a *"Being Of Awareness", [not a Being WITH awareness, but a Being OF Awareness],* allows us to see that *The UFO* very well indeed represents, visually in symbolical form, the *true Man, The Man* as a *Being OF Awareness; fast and fluid, aerial and ever pervasive, trans-medium we surely are, as a Being, Of, Awareness.*

The most puzzling and paradoxical concepts, are revealed to be but aspects of *"The Man"* himself; that, *Man* has always struggled, and continues ever more-so today, to stand in front of a mirror.

Mr. Jung is adamant, in that the more we hide from ourselves, the larger the burst from the proverbially notorious *"unconscious"*. That, *literally*, you shall be haunted by your own Self, in *whatever horror you've already pre-conceptualized for yourself* in ignorance, for we are just now beginning to uncover and discover the truth of our own selves and what we truly are as creatures, *Things, Of* Awareness. We in truth are just as *unidentified* as *The UFO*, which summarizes everything pretty well I suppose.

> *Undeterred by rationalistic criticism, it thrusts itself to the fore-front in the form of a symbolic rumor, accompanied and reinforced by the appropriate visions, and thus activates an archetype that has always expressed order, deliverance, salvation, and wholeness. It is characteristic of our time that the archetype, in contrast to its previous manifestations, should now take the form of an object, a technological construction, in order to avoid the odiousness of mythological personification. Anything that looks technological goes down without difficulty with modern man.*
>
> C. Jung|Flying Saucers

We must consider that we have a majority of humanity attempting to reside in a world, a *Paracosm*, of what they have *preconceived* to be filled with traditional *UFO activity*, unaware that while they fear and hope for these preconceived travelers, this same paracosm harbors a bigger game. A wider-reality in which *The UFO* is naught more than a concept used by *men-of-deception* to fuel their own agendas, as men of power have done from the very dawn of himself...*this is how it has always been.*

Ancient men of power, allowed and accepted the *spirits,* the *gods, any and all that would increase their power and reach.* And, they shall always hide and fear from those they cannot control or erase.

The UFO is valuable to those who seek to control the masses, just as the ancient temple of the god [*where, unsurprisingly, only the king could meet "face to face" with this god*], ...always pacified the people with its awe and majesty. The majority understood it not, thus *trusted the concepts of another child with gold around his neck.*

Children on a playground, each and all independently naive of the wider, greater, collective truth, that of a more-grand reality encompassing all of these games and concepts. One in which *The UFO* is but a sort of peek-a-boo game the *"higher"* [*read: more developed; evolved*] Self-Awareness tickles and teases, like a trickster, the *"lower"* animal-awareness, therefore initiating and encouraging *a chase*, that you might grow the Awareness to become that which you see, the proverbial *Alien* that, you are.

For, a *Being Of Awareness, aware of itself as such, is truly Alien to this beautiful blue planet. Look around.*

Man opens his mortal animal eyes to see a body reflected in a pool of still water, subsequently realizing he *has a mind which directs this image of a body,* only to then be haunted by yet another aspect to *The Trinity that he is,* until, he accepts that *that* which haunts his body and mind, is, simply, *himself; his own Self.*

The Awareness that he is, which his animal body and mind *both sense and detect* and, attempt to relay [*bring to consciousness*] to the awaiting *Man* [Higher/Hybrid-Awareness] on standby, until the ignorant ruler of this kingdom that *The Man* as a Being Of Awareness is, decides to acknowledge and accept what he could never possibly *"see"* on his own: *his own Self, for his Self is invisible and fluid when in motion, like that of The UFO.*

Somehow our consciousness is at odds with our genetic inheritance. When it comes to life and death it seems we don't agree, and that could be the result of consciousness coming rather late to the party.
DeLonge, Levenda|Sekret Machines, Man

It is impossible to see reality except by looking through the eyes of the Party. That is the fact that you have got to relearn, Winston. It needs an act of self-destruction, an effort of the will. You must humble yourself before you can become sane.
G. Orwell|1984

The Man sees naught but by reflection, and the body and mind which join to form this true Man, the *Being Of Awareness,* reflect to *each other always* their own animalistic, archetypal *observations*/perceptions/sensations, which become ever the more literal an awareness, a concept of, *The Awareness that is the New Man they each form by uniting.* Thus, what *Man* refuses to acknowledge and *see,* is that *body and mind sense "an alien presence"* [*the Higher Self-Awareness that "hovers above" both, as the Hybrid creation it surely is*] and join, forming the symbol of wholeness, completion, and Jungian individuation, attempting to bring to you, *The Awareness,* literally, *their own sense of your sense;* a confusing feedback loop of sorts. An awareness of one's own Awareness.

Father and Mother have awareness of Baby, before Baby is birthed.

A mind and body acknowledgment of, your own existence.

We mustn't doubt our evolved capabilities any longer, for there is nothing, absolutely nothing, that a self-aware being cannot have awareness of, as a Being Of Awareness himself.

There is naught we can't traverse or penetrate, precisely as *The UFO* attempts to show to us. *The speed of quantum thought,* for a damned good reason. We must forget our old concepts of *"real", "material", "unreal"* and *"spiritual".* We successfully divided nature, *that we might grasp it;* we must now *reunite our supposed opposite concepts into the One reality we now know it to have actually been from the beginning.*

The Creation [*read: conceptualization*] of "Man", considering the true Man to not be body nor mind, but a creature of naught but ethereal Awareness:

> *"And God said, Let us"* [*us* = the many separate processes of mind and body, ruled overall by the aspects we label Masculine & Feminine, or, Left-Brain & Right-Brain] *"make man in our"* [hybrid of Male/Female, Left/Right joined together, as One; psychologically we conceptualize many separate aspects of "The Self", coming together under the Jungian process of Individuation, or, Wholeness] *"image, after our likeness"* [*likeness,* as in, a concept, an awareness of, yet *not those,* of both mind and body]: *"and let them"* [the Man, a concept, a new thing we can label a, "Being Of Awareness"] *"have dominion over the fish of the sea and over the*

fowl of the air, and over the cattle and over all the earth, and over
every creeping thing that creepeth upon the earth."
Genesis 1:26|KJV

This verse, accurately describes *both, The UFO, as well as the actual and*
true "Man", a Being Of Awareness. The Man is, has always been, simply a
Concept, within the garden of the "Unconscious". Like the other concepts already
mentioned in this conversation, your idea of the "Unconscious" must also
evolve.

Man, itself a concept *charged with stewardship* of this primarily internal,
magical place.

It would seem, perhaps, that the supposed UFO occupants have also read
the Christian Bible [necessarily so, if we accept *The UFO* as *The Man*]: *"...have*
dominion over the fish of the sea and over the fowl of the air, and over the cattle
and over all the earth, and over every creeping thing that creepeth upon the earth."
Again, Carl Jung:

> *"According to the rumour... They are beings who are carrying out*
> *a cautious survey of the earth...or, more menacingly, are spying out*
> *landing places with a view to settling the population of a planet that*
> *has got into difficulties..."*

In short, we may find much more value, in fact *"gold"*, by reconsidering the
concept of *The UFO*, as naught but *the attempted visualization, the attempted*
conceptualization and thus "conscious-ization" of, "The Self". Mankind evolving,
becoming ever more aware of his own more-true Self as, a dead-alive cosmic
"thing" called *Awareness.*

This necessarily can and should be extrapolated, in the sense that a *group* or
collective of "Selves" have the same potential to become aware of *their greater*
"collective-self", [here I am considering such times as a group of war-ships at
sea, together, alone and isolated, they surely have "separated" from the greater
mass-of-humanity and, formed a "new", if not temporary, collective-awareness,
which modern Man, as a Being OF Awareness, surely encounters and attempts
to conceptualize; "become aware of ", ie, bring-into consciousness/incorporate into

itself.] For, the evolved concept of *The Man* accepts, that *The Man* is itself naught but *Awareness of its own Self as Awareness,* therefore his Self *being Awareness,* is *necessarily entangled in a quantum web with all else.* There is nothing the *Man* cannot become aware of and incorporate into this *Awareness* that he himself, in fullness and truth, *is.*

It is, simply, the *innocently ignorant individual manifestation of such infor-mation,* which remains the outstanding "issue".

As *Man* begins to accept that he indeed sees naught but his own reflection, individually and collectively, *The Alien "craft" necessarily departs, and is not seen from again,* for *The Man* has incorporated back, *that* which he gave away so long ago, *his own sovereignty...in fact, himself.*

> *The cause must strike at the roots of our existence if it is to explain such an extraordinary phenomenon as the UFOs.*
>
> C. Jung|Flying Saucers

The very *idea* of *UFO* and *UAP* is, already outdated.

We must accept that anything yet *unidentified* and actually profane is, pur-posefully so [*unidentified*].

There are no more acceptable excuses for the modern Man to have any actual material objects floating and buzzing around him not yet catalogued and documented. Most today remain within an ancient mindset of supposed *Disclosure,* yet awaiting the laughable "*official*" word from their ancient-mind-ed government, not realizing they may now grow their own Self [*Awareness*], beyond these ancient and tired states-of-mind.

The UFO is a symbol of freedom.

> *Raja Yoga does not, after the unpardonable manner of some mod-ern scientists, deny the existence of facts which are difficult to ex-plain; on the other hand, it gently yet in no uncertain terms tells the superstitious that miracles and answers to prayers, and powers of faith, though true as facts, are not rendered comprehensible through the superstitious explanation of attributing them to the agency of a being, or beings, above the clouds.*

It declares that each man is only a conduit for the infinite ocean of knowledge and power that lies behind mankind. It teaches that desires and wants are in man, that the power of supply is also in man; and that wherever and whenever a desire, a want, a prayer has been fulfilled, it was out of this infinite magazine that the supply came, and not from any supernatural being. The idea of supernatural beings may rouse to a certain extent the power of action in man, but it also brings spiritual decay. It brings dependence; it brings fear; it brings superstition. It degenerates into a horrible belief in the natural weakness of man.

Swami Vivekananda|Raja Yoga

Other children on this giant playground shall always seek to control you, *with their own malnourished ideas.*

Man, from the beginning, has attempted to manifest, *create externally*, with his ape-like hands, what he first feels, intuits, *conceptualizes...internally.*

Man, unaware of his own fullness and truth of what he is, has always visualized *"things in the sky"*, and then sought to re-create such *visions*, that he may then in-turn, *chase those same visualizations* he senses to be *"in the sky"*, not knowing how to express the reality that *the sky is naught but a blank canvas for his own projected Self-Awareness.*

Man fails to accept the ancient spiritual knowledge that, he awakens to observe the battles and cosmic happenings of *his own body and mind come-together.* That modern Man continues to identify his own Self with *one or the other, either body, or mind*, not yet accepting the reality that he is paradoxically *neither and both.* That *Man is the hybrid creation long prophesied by the many supposed "alien abductor" and "fairy" of old.*

The crowning revelation is that "though he (the Gnostic) is in the world, moves in the world, he is not of the world, he does not belong to it, but he comes and is from elsewhere." The Mandaean Right-hand Ginza reveals to him: "Thou art not from here, thy root is not of the world". And the Left-hand Ginza: "Thou comest not from here, thy stock is not hence; thy place is the place of Life." And we read in the Book of John: "I am a man of the Other World."

As we have seen, Indian philosophical speculation...takes a similar position. The Self (purusha) is essentially a "stranger" and has nothing to do with the World. As Isvara Krishna writes, the Self (the Spirit) "is alone, indifferent, a mere inactive spectator" in the drama of Life and History.

M. Eliade|Myth and Reality

Man, from the very beginning, *is "The Hybrid"*.
The Awareness, the proverbial *"spark"*, *"The User"* and *"Experiencer"* of *both mind and body as One "system"*. Hardware (Right) and Software (Left) uniting to form *the experience, the awareness.*

In another way, we can see this biologically as the *Left and Right Hemispheres of the animal brain, coming into union to form an "Awareness" of each-other, and the ensuing struggle of both, to control The Hybrid baby formed by that union, which we are.* We feel, and see daily, our own and all others' struggle to balance Mind with Body; Spirit with Matter; Black with White; Up with Down; In with Out; Hardware with Software; and the rarity with which we actually encounter those whom have harmonized their own system into "wholeness", which is naturally of course, simply, *balance.*

Human consciousness is something they want out of the way. It seems to interfere with their plans.

DeLonge, Levenda|Sekret Machines, Man

—*Resnik*

Well all the words that I've been reading
Have now started the act of bleeding
Into one, into one

Collective Soul|The World I Know

The sphere expresses the soul germ. The four rayed circle with a central point expresses the spiritual soul.

Dr. H. Baraduc|The Human Soul

***

RESNIK,

Wow. I mean... I just don't even have time to think about all this...*stuff? Data?*

There seems to be a lot of information tied-up together, just like the concepts of *Consciousness* and *UFO*. Well, regardless, thanks for the info. I'll get around to it eventually, maybe.

Just keeping it as real as I know how to.

—[*Insert your name here.*]

4

NO SPOON

SEEKER,

Time itself, is but a concept.

It is as subject to alteration and evolution as any and all concepts. It may be suspended if we desire it to be, *or altogether forgotten.* We may speed it up or in fact slow it down. We see this with each shift-of-the-clock during supposed "daylight savings", as *time* is naught but an intellectual tool; a *concept,* devised to assist Man in *dividing The Day,* "Day" being, *Life,* that we might conquer it, thus our own nature.

Information cannot in truth be tied, for *tied* itself is but a word, a symbol, pointing toward, *something...another concept.*

Rather than conceptually tying *supposedly separate* concepts together precariously, we may evolve them into one-another and see that "*information*" leads to a development of a concept, that of "time", that "time" is not separate from *information*. Time, is in fact *a collection of information, joined to form a concept, that of Time itself.*

Time is nothing to be "*grasped*", thus in this sense, for one to "*believe*" in and employ the concept of *Time,* it should be relatively easy to also "*believe*" in *many other concepts that cannot be physically grasped, to include the proverbial Soul, which many of us now feel to be much more palpable and "real" than this idea of "time", which so easily shifts to accommodate capitalist work-forces.*

The reality is indeed that, *Time is real when or if we need it,* yet within us individually and collectively there is no such truth, for *Time is an assemblage of data come-together to form an Idea.* There is no "time" as you currently understand it, in *The Cosmos.*

There is no beginning nor shall there be an end. We see that all merely transmutes, and the further we look "*in*" or "*back*", we see but more and more increasing levels of both simplicity and complexity; beauty and horror. The closer we look, the further away we appear to be from any actual answer, and yet the answer is there before us if we choose to accept it. A never-beginning, never-ending, swirling ouroboros mass of both light and dark that is at once alive and dead, life and death, nothing and everything, all at once, and the sooner we realize and accept this, the sooner we may embrace our actual potential as *a species of cosmic-awareness.*

We employ any and all concepts we require, while in the *"space"* of pure awareness, meaning, we can employ *the Idea of "Time" when we contemplate, meditate* or engage in extra-sensory activities such as *Remote-Viewing* and the like, to assist in our *"world building"* or *"seeking of information"* for specific periods and experiences. Yet, it remains simply a concept, which we may alter instantly in that "place", for we are always the rulers of our own domains.

In short, *Time* is relevant if we want it to be, *internally or externally,* and if we do *not* require its use, then *Time is irrelevant.*

Time is a concept we use to survive externally, this survival does not necessarily apply internally. Inside, when we contemplate or *Remote-View*, we do so with the knowledge of truth that there is *"no spoon"..."no time"*, and that if there were, *it were only because we deemed it so, and it shall bend if we so damn desire it to,* whether a metal spoon or the ancient concept of Time itself.

If it helps in our seeking of information, we may employ the concept of *Time* by *imagining information to be "tied" to it,* yet this is only a tool, a method, helpful yet *not at all necessary,* for *The Awareness* that we in truth actually are, *instantly knows who, what, when, where, how,* and any *other relevant details* we deem necessary. It is only *our failure to recognize this information for what it is* when it arrives, that is of issue here. This is what we must now work to develop, *easily and quickly done once we begin to re-conceptualize what it means to be "The Man".*

—Resnik

> *Can you blame me for not wanting both feet*
> *On the ground*
> *While you follow routine and waste your days*
> *I'm in the clouds Raining down*
> *This is all ours to fuck with*

This is all ours to taunt
This is our home, our stomping ground
What's stopping us?
What's stopping us?
What's stopping us?

Low Roar|The Painter

5

PARACOSMIC EXPRESSION

SEEKER,

I am reminded of the *Paracosm*:

> *"Paracosm, is a detailed imaginary world. Paracosms are thought generally to originate in childhood and to have one or numerous creators. The creator of a paracosm has a complex and deeply felt relationship with this subjective universe, which may incorporate real-world or imaginary characters and conventions. Commonly having its own geography, history, and language, it is an experience that is often developed during childhood and continues over a long period of time, months or even years, as a sophisticated reality that can last into adulthood."*

Now, [*We*]*kipedia* goes-on to state much more about the concept of a *Paracosm*, to include:

> *"...paracosm play is recognized as one of the indicators of a high level of creativity, which educators now realize is as important as intelligence."*

I see, we are each children who develop our own *Paracosm* while still very young, and carry this forward with us *throughout life*.

Considering that the internal "world", is the primary "swamp" in which "The Man" ascends from to greet the light, *the awareness* of life that he is, it would be the case indeed that externally, in the "outside world" of materiality, we each are, in a sense, an expression, a projection of, each-others inner reality.

Extrapolating the fact that we are all the same, *connected to the same universal source of "everything and all"*, then naturally our *individual Paracosms* surely differ only slightly, just as we each wear *"unique" styles of clothing*, and yet underlying it all *is the same One collective-awareness we each are a part of.*

> *...but on the whole the Neverlands have a family resemblance, and if they stood still in a row you could say of them that they have each other's nose, and so forth. On these magic shores children at play are for ever beaching their coracles. We too have been there; we can still hear the sound of the surf...*
>
> J.M. Barrie|Peter Pan

You can say that, *The Man*, [that new being *of* awareness], necessarily *must build his Paracosm from a young age indeed*, in that *Man* is a creature *who resides within this Paracosm* his whole "life".

Paracosm...evolve the concept. Realize, an imaginary world is made possible necessarily *because we are, imaginary creatures; creatures of imagination.* Creatures, capable of creating these imaginary realms to begin with. Evolve the concept. Imaginary *does not belong bundled together with our ancient concept of "unreal".*

Realize, we *imagine, because we are a creature of imagination.*

Our true world, if we so choose to accept, now, is the co-called imaginary realm. Your paracosm is, as real as you are. You are the divine creator of *your own imaginary realm*...you need not your body nor your mind any longer *when, you liberate your "Self" from their ancient soil.*

What of the Collective Paracosm of Mankind? What of the Collective Paracosm of a, Military? What of each Individual Paracosm of each Man, embedded within these greater collective-imaginings?

Now we get to the intuition of *alternate and parallel dimensions, bubble-realities within other realities, simulation-theory, etc.* For, when we evolve the concept of *The Man*, we *accept all these theories as the One truth they reveal: that each Man is necessarily a portal to both his own Paracosm, and that of The Whole.*

Many realities intertwined, within the One system we label "Cosmos", a concept evolved now to *include* our ancient concepts of profane *and* spirit, visible *and* invisible, for each are but sides to the greater, rapidly rotating coin that is *Life*. An Ouroboros of light and dark that, *when perceived appropriately and balanced, shimmers invitingly, glowing in harmonious stability;* neither blinding, nor without heat; a soft, illuminating radiance that melts away ancient, frozen chaff.

—*Resnik*

> *The "World", then, is always the world that one knows and in which one lives; it differs from one type of culture to another; hence there are a considerable number of "Worlds".*

M. Eliade|Myth and Reality

6

LIVING, MINDED

SEEKER,

Our technology and creativity today, can assist in our conceptualizing this "new world" we find ourselves discussing and embarking upon and in.

As we may "pull down" our Virtual Reality visor over our mortal eyes, [instantly leaving our body essentially behind], to enter an entirely new "imaginary" digital game realm, built for many users to interact with and play within, all at once...*meditation is this same, albeit very natural and organic, act*...in that, *Man* closes his mortal eyes and is thus charged with godlike creative responsibility to, not just participate in another designed game, but *to build and create his own inner world.*

Within this inner world one may very rapidly create. You may imagine a simple wooden door, upon which opening, allows easy and fluid access into a *"storeroom of cosmic data"*.

Man has, from the beginning, given away his own sovereignty to outside actors. Thus *Man* may, simply, *quickly, in the flash of a moment, take-back his own authority,* and approach this *storeroom of cosmic data* knowing that he is now returned home...that, this *room of information* which is the proverbial *"unconscious", in fact birthed him, thus always welcomes him home.* [Remember, you must evolve your current concept of "unconscious" to intend something like, "Everything I am not currently conscious of." The "Un"-conscious, so-called, is *not* unconscious, *you are. The Unconscious,* in truth, *harbors the hyperactive Consciousness of all and everything.* You, are a secretion of this everything, as a newborn baby is a secretion of its mother: Mommy dearest is hyper aware of her child, while the child is aware of little more than the breast from which it seeks nourishment.

Man must get out of his own way, *by accepting his own evolved divine capabilities. Man is as much The Cosmos as The Cosmos.* He is that. Man is divine, godly indeed; *as much god as he's imagined for any other external Alien overlord or White-bearded old Man.*

When we meditate, we do so with a *knowing* that we are truly home, and that, what remains dark or unknown, is so, *simply and necessarily because we have yet to illumine it;* yet to decorate; yet to outfit with whatever we see fit, and that this giant room of information shall morph and respond to our cosmic willpower. You are encouraged, Seeker, to *humbly, sincerely,* yet *boldly* and *proudly* command this imagined room of cosmic information as you command your own Self, for the truth remains, that *all* becomes known *when we accept and finally see, our own damn Self as the divine "Thing" we in fact are.*

Surely, there is not a government yet in this world that would encourage this sort of Self-seeking and development. *Contrarily,* each would withhold no tactic to *ensure Man remains clumsily and stupidly "hot on the trail" of the ubiquitous UFO filled with "visitors from Alpha Centauri".*

When we meditate, we do so *knowing* there is naught we cannot *instantly* perceive, *visualize, hear,* especially and specifically *when done so with an intention of "Love",* which itself is yet another concept in desperate need of *evolution,* for there is naught that will not be affected as we begin to re-write our story, beginning with the very cornerstone concept, that of, *"The Man".* You cringe, or foolishly wet yourself, upon hearing the word, *love,* only because you've yet to evolve your very ancient idea of "it".

That, *reality itself shifts* before your mortal eyes, necessarily so, when you tear-down the tired idea of *Man,* and build anew a modern concept of *"The Man",* incorporating each and all the pieces we have already uncovered and discovered. Everything.

All, evolves...we needn't *wait* for our ancient idea of "science" to also evolve.

What is acceptable now, "today", *always changes, always grows or gets left aside.*

We intuit our *collective-connection to each-other;* we intuit more to this supposed reality than science can educate us on, thus, we take what we know and *"fast forward", "skip ahead";* concepts we can deploy to our advantage now, by accepting that science and the *men-of-letter* reside in their own Paracosm, and we "common men" needn't wait for these ancients to evolve, *that we may leapfrog these dying breeds and become something new and independent altogether.*

We are, if we accept for ourselves, *our own government now*. Just ask Edward Carpenter.

If the ancient concept refuses to evolve, so-be-it, *but we needn't retard our own Self-growth and maturation, in anticipation of this ancient "giant" known as Government*; for we may *press ahead individually*, securing our own future independently, knowing the greater-truth of our undeniable and unavoidable ultimate connection to one-another, for this is surely the next logical step in our evolutionary growth as a species: *the growth of the individual*, himself whole and balanced and capable of then turning around to grab-hold of each and all others he can, *that together we then re-unite as liberated and whole individuated Beings, come-together as the One they had always been*, yet remained darkly confused about, separate and warlike, competitive and survival-minded, rather than individual and love-like. Not competitive but *reflective*. Not survival-minded but *living, minded*.

—*Resnik*

7

CLEAR JELL-O

But it is our expression that there are no positive differences: that all things are like a mouse and a bug in the heart of a cheese. They're there a week, or they stay there a month: both are then only transmutations of cheese. I think we're all bugs and mice, and are only different expressions of an all-inclusive cheese.

C. Fort|The Book of The Damned

SEEKER,

I remind myself that, when meditating or visualizing or, otherwise connecting with "the all", "*in that space*" [*that is at once myself*], there is no concept of time other than that which I bring with me. That, simply, there is *no time or space in the realm of cosmic, collective-awareness*, thus, *perceiving "future" events, is not seeing the future, but an ever present awareness of, now.*

There is no "time-travel". *Man, brings time to its knees, and to his own feet. Time, travels to The Man, not the other-way around.*

What at first may seem confusing or difficult to grasp may end up being more simple than we at first conceptualize. We cannot think as small-minded animals of a single planet. We must imagine vastly "larger"; *expanded.*

That our own supposed future, *is but the past for an even vastly more futuristic [future] "humanity"*, as our own apparent past *was the future long prophesied by* [ancient] *"humanity".*

All, has always been *an endless string of a single cosmic-happening, observed from infinite points that is at once the happening itself.*

We reside in a cosmic jell-o of sorts. Charles Fort preferred cheese.

Mobile, but effectively *anchored within what we call "space"*. All in this "space", connected by an apparently invisible, clear "gelatin-like substance" known as, Awareness. The darkest of matter. So clear, it appears dark. So dark and clear, you might even call it an "anti-matter".

We can forget the ancient idea of *Time*, which seeks to divide always, and toss it aside, *that all division reunites as the atom smashing into itself, and allow the heat and illumination from this reuniting to bring awareness of all and every to this very exact moment,* for it is all at once unfolding; it has already unfolded, we are simply at this particular point, ignorantly stuck in our jell-o.

If we close our eyes and allow *The Awareness we are*, to slide and glide within this cosmic jell-o, we see *it touches any and all, at all times, has always been here, covering earth, each event and movement leaving scratches and markings within this jell-o that our Self-Awareness may read like a book; like a wall-of-data; a realm of language as Mr. McKenna might suggest;* for our new concept of *The Man* proclaims, we are in fact *that* jell-o.

We are *that*; we are *that awareness always connected.*

From the beginning, *The Awareness that we are*, [that we now individuate from to maneuver within at will], *was there*. Awareness; consciousness, is the magical dark substance "holding" all supposed other material together.

—*Resnik*

Tempest-tossed souls, wherever ye may be, under whatsoever conditions ye may live, know this in the ocean of life the isles of Blessedness are smiling, and the sunny shore of your ideal awaits your coming. Keep your hand firmly upon the helm of thought. In the bark of your soul reclines the commanding Master; He does but sleep: wake Him. Self-control is strength; Right Thought is mastery; Calmness is power. Say unto your heart, "Peace, be still!"

J. Allen|As A Man Thinketh

8

GUIDE AND CONTROL

SEEKER,

Considering *The Phenomenon*, is in fact simply *Man*, yet we remain unaware of our own awareness, we fail to see that *The Phenomenon does* represent a *"higher-intelligence" or "guiding-consciousness", that of our very own,* which seeks, [as it has always done from the very beginning], to guide and control humanity into its own "future".

That the Tree of Life *that is awareness*, might be fruitful and *multiply!*

Imagine the true organism of Mankind *not as an organism of mere flesh*. Imagine the *invisible mass* of *collective-awareness hovering above that animal meat.* That *collective-consciousness* is a tree, literally the tree of life, that like all trees, has been growing itself that it might produce its very own fruit within the body of each human. Why? The same reason any tree produces fruit, *for the survival of the species.* In our case, a new species of Awareness; an "Aware-Thing", or, "Thing, OF Awareness."

We must be aware of *the new concept of The Man*, in that this tree and fruit we speak of is the new cosmic creature that we are, *a Being OF Self-Awareness...*for our species is not the simple biological-machine called animal, *for the species we are, is a species of Awareness.*

Surely *the Self-Aware "Alien" that is the new hybrid "thing" here on Earth called, The Man*, is unique in his ability to recognize *"giants"*, [*not just the mass-movements-of-collective-animal-meat, but more importantly the hovering collective-consciousness of all*]. We will very quickly see that *Man* is the *new thing* evolved here, and that we have never truly been alone, if not absolutely unique, in this corner of the cosmos, with our *Individuated-Self-Awareness.*

It becomes apparent very quickly that, considering any Government of the world has actually for a moment taken this topic *seriously*, the truth is less about "extraterrestrial visitor", and everything to do with *Man and what he is, thus his capabilities and abilities.*

The only true and actual conspiracy worthy of our attention, remains *the conspiracy of Government against the Individual, that, there is naught any government, any king, any CEO fears more than the awareness of the common Man. For when the common Man embraces his potential, embraces his evolution, he quickly sees he has rapidly leapfrogged that tired institution of control over animals, known as government.*

Indeed, as I have said elsewhere, it shall take our own sort of insanity, embracing our supposed *"crazy"*, to overcome this animal-farm we call modern society and governance.

—*Resnik*

> *To fight the Empire is to be infected by it's derangement. This is a paradox; whoever defeats a segment of the Empire becomes the Empire; it proliferates like a virus, imposing its form on its enemies. Thereby it becomes its enemies.*
>
> P.K. Dick|VALIS

9

META-MATERIAL

Men have spent enormous amounts of time, energy and money on the finding, mining and cutting of colored pebbles. Why? The utilitarian can offer no explanation...But as soon as we take into account the facts of visionary experience, everything becomes clear. In vision, men perceive a profusion of what Ezekiel calls "stones of fire"...These things are self-luminous, exhibit a preternatural brilliance of color and possess a preternatural significance. The material objects which most nearly resemble these sources of visionary illumination are gem stones. To acquire such a stone is to acquire something whose preciousness is guaranteed by the fact that it exists in the Other World.

A. Huxley|The Doors Of Perception

...holding a certain efficient combination of metals in his hands, would automatically drop into the somnambulistic state. The same result could be obtained if the subject put his feet on metal plates or sheets.

E.J. Dingwall|Abnormal Hypnotic Phenomena

SEEKER,

I look at the [now ancient] story of *"recovered materials"*, in this way:

[!] *Deception;* in that, to deny the abilities and capabilities of Mankind today is foolish, and to deny the very reality of self or externally-imposed deception is even more-so. We know enough, *now*, to know, Mankind is not only capable of producing these meta-materials, he most assuredly would do so *secretively*.

And,

[!] *Man*, not knowing himself accurately, unaware of his own capabilities and abilities, unaware of his own awareness and the potential of *that* which he in fact is, unaware of his cosmic-connection and ability to will what he shall, that he might continue forward into the abyss we label "future", shall be blind when "help" arrives. And what I mean by that is, *Remote Viewing, Ingo Swann, Prof. Dean Radin, Stanford University, Russel Targ, the Yoga Sutras of Patanjali, etc.* So many "voices" which proclaim: *Man can obtain information at will, when he humbly and sincerely seeks for it.* Thus, Mankind now approaches a moment where its apparent survival depends on obtaining the ability to travel outward into the vast universe, and *this would require unique and rare materials unknown to previous generations of individual Man, only because they hadn't known to yet seek for them.*

We must consider that this has happened many times indeed. *Ancient-Man*, at one point in "history" had need for a new material, unknown to exist...yet on one fine magical day, he was guided, led to a deposit of, *Gold...or Iron...or Silver...or, Plutonium!*

This to say, that *Man guides himself, with a symbol of his own Self* [*The Circle*], *to deposits of new elements* that, unknown to Man heretofore, have been within the crust of the Earth from the very beginning.

Man must realize that all remains dark and hidden and "impossible", *only until he becomes aware of it.* That, "bacteria" had always been present in rotten or uncooked foods, yet Man had not awareness of it until very recently indeed.

Man knew not anything at all, *until, he did.*

That, where the ancient minded say "*impossible*", the more-aware Self, as the god it is, says, "*Hold my beer and step aside.*"

> *...people felt they were being observed and spied upon from space.*
> C. Jung|Flying Saucers

If we accept *The UFO* as a projection of the *Self*, [yourself, as a creature or thing not of flesh but of an invisible, ethereal "force" we call Awareness]; then we can harness this information and accept that perhaps the unusual flight patterns of *The UFO* resemble the signals of insects attempting to alert the Hive to some very valuable source of food; *some new resource.*

That *The UFO,* being a symbol of a much *"Higher" or more-developed Awareness,* "above" that of the mere animal mind, *alerts the manimal* to what it has now detected and become aware of; the Self works constantly to lead the *manimal* onward and forward, thus *The UFO flashes and shimmers over a portion of the earth which it detects a valuable resource,* a *"meta-material"*, or any other valuable life-giving, energetic resources. Resources, that have very more likely than not, *always been there,* for eons of our concept of time, *just now popping-into the awareness that is the newly awakening, more evolved Man.*

We knew not *oil* would spout forth from the earth we walk upon, until, *one day it just happened.* The same is taking place here. Man has enlightened himself as to the presence of these meta-materials here in our own backyard, and there are those Men of greed and deception who have already long ago begun deconstructing and reconstructing in their own likeness, their own meta-materials.

Man is more divine and godly than we admit, and yet there are those in laboratories who already embrace their potential as divine *creators.*

Simply, accepting the reality of "Extra Sensory Perception", or "Anomalous Mental Phenomena", and evolving the concept, we see that *The UFO* [that is our *Self*], *may alert and show us those "things/sights/areas"* we must become aware of. We see the, now dated, news that *The UFO* apparently has an affinity for *"Nuclear Sights";* this should be obvious, in that we are in fact aware of our very own advanced-awareness of *both danger and potential, posed by these nuclear-filled energetic sites like power-stations, and machines like Navy submarines.*

> *Their flight, accordingly, resembles that of a flying insect.*
> C. Jung|Flying Saucers

We see naught above our nuclear facilities and military congregations than *our very own awareness,* for these sights are *necessarily under very high-aware security-awareness already, and filled with highly-aware and alert individuals, trained to be ever more-so alert and vigilant;* we thus create a swirling ouroboros of hyper awareness that, we absolutely *become aware of, as Beings Of Awareness ourselves.*

We mustn't fear or deny what we perceive, we must simply incorporate these sightings into a much greater and expanded *concept of Reality and The Man itself.*

We continue to march forward into "the future", with an ancient concept of what this all is, *this thing we call, Life.* Of-course nothing today seems to make any sense, and questions only beget more questions, for we set out from the very beginning, with a false foundation of our own Self.

—*Resnik*

In the first case an objectively real, physical process forms the basis for an accompanying myth; in the second case an archetype creates the corresponding vision. To these two causal relationships we must add a third possibility, namely, that of a "synchronistic", i.e., acausal, meaningful coincidence— a problem that has occupied men's minds ever since the time of Geulincx, Leibniz, and Schopenhauer. It is an hypothesis that has special bearing on phenomena connected with archetypal psychic processes.

C. Jung|Flying Saucers

The influence of the metals on the human body was always, in Robiano's experience, instantaneous and infallibly the same, never even for a single moment changing in its effect or results.

E.J. Dingwall|Abnormal Hypnotic Phenomena

10

FIGHT-CLUB CONSCIOUSNESS

...I have urged that the psyche be recognized as having its own peculiar reality.

C. Jung|Flying Saucer

SEEKER,

Consider here that, we, *together*, collectively, are a *"higher intelligence"* and greater-awareness which many have encountered during some, yet not all, of the ubiquitous *Alien* encounter scenarios.

Imagine the human animal, before it evolved what we conceptualize to be *self awareness; Self Consciousness; [For surely there were humans here anatomically identical to the Modern Man, yet lacking the glow of Self Awareness]*. Now, imagine the reality of today, in which we have a *majority* of humanity still catching up, lagging behind with a "low-level" [read: lesser developed] awareness of themselves, *completely in "the dark" and unaware of their own greater potential for growth*.

Fear and Arrogance seem to be preventing the children of men *today*, from accepting this of themselves, preferring to reside in their own Paracosm, *designed and forged by the minds of their ancients, and passed-down to them from generation to generation*.

Only the fearless today will *destroy this ancient castle to build anew their own "kingdom"*. Why I indeed express in writing that, *it shall take "crazy"*, the *"craziest"* of us, *to rise to the top of an already insane litter of monkeys*.

We must think differently, or always risk the almost unavoidable slide, back into the illusion of the pack, the ancient collective paracosm constructed by fearful minded manimals.

In just these cases the unconscious has to resort to particularly drastic measures in order to make its contents perceived. It does this most vividly by projection, by extrapolating its contents into an object, which then reflects back what had previously lain hidden in the unconscious.

C. Jung|Flying Saucers

We can consider the possibility that, *within the Collective-Paracosm created by fearful animal-minded men*, we give-away our own sovereignty to that of an *Other, an Alien force that we charge with providing* [*and therefore expect to receive*], *saving-grace for humanity.*

We know, that any individual mind may divide itself into many different *avatars, personalities, and characters,* especially in times of stress and anxiety, in effort to accomplish tasks or consider facts that the normal, waking, lesser-developed concept-of-self [ego], could never possibly entertain without psychologically breaking.

So too, does the *Collective-Mind of Mankind* go about charging *divided aspects of its own Self,* those *Paracosmic Aliens,* with agency. Literally imbuing these very real, yet very imagined aspects of our own greater Collective-Self, with the *Soul of the Creator* [read: *Us, the Collective Of Awareness*], that those discarnate aspects of our greater-collective-mind may then *unilaterally act-out and upon The Man, for that was and is their sole responsibility and charge, to lead Mankind "un"consciously, darkly, the way it cannot yet lead itself consciously in the light.*

Angels, demons, gods, jinn, Small Grays, Tall Nordics, Reptillians, insectoids, humanoids...aren't they all just machines, devices we've created as drones (as unmanned psychological vehicles) to penetrate into hidden realms of our own consciousness?

DeLonge, Levenda|Sekret Machines, Man

While she slept she had a dream. She dreamt that the Neverland had come too near and that a strange boy had broken through from it. He did not alarm her, for she thought she had seen him before in the faces of many women who have no children. Perhaps he is to be found in the faces of some mothers also. But in her dream he had rent the film that obscures the Neverland, and she saw Wendy and John and Michael peeping through the gap. The dream by itself would have been a trifle, but while she was dreaming the window of the nursery blew open, and a boy did drop on the floor. He was accompanied by a strange light, no bigger than your fist, which darted about the room like a living thing, and I think it must have been this light that wakened Mrs. Darling.

J.M. Barrie|Peter Pan

You can also imagine the film, or the novel it is based upon written by Chuck Palahniuk, known as *"Fight Club"*, in which one character divides himself, *that he might accomplish and live how he cannot allow and accept for himself yet consciously.* Consider *The Alien* as the necessary Tyler Durden to humanity's childish, fearful, animal Narrator inside which still lacks the new concept of what he actually is...both at once.

—*Resnik*

The discovery of unconscious psychic processes more than fifty years ago is still far from being common knowledge and its implications are still not recognized. Modern man still does not realize that he is entirely dependent on the co-operation of the unconscious, which can actually cut short the very next sentence he proposes to speak. He is unaware that he is continuously sustained by something, while all the time he regards himself exclusively as the doer. He depends on and is sustained by an entity he does not know, but of which he has intimations that "occurred" to—or, as we can more fitly say, revealed themselves to—long-forgotten forbears in the grey dawn of history.

Whence did they come? Obviously from the unconscious processes, from that so-called unconscious which still precedes consciousness in every new human life, as the mother precedes the child. The unconscious depicts itself in dreams and visions, as it always did, holding before us images which, unlike the fragmented functions of consciousness, emphasize facts that relate to the unknown whole man, and only apparently to the function which interests us to the exclusion of all else. Although dreams usually speak the language of our particular specialism...they refer to the whole, or at the very least to what man also is, namely the utterly dependent creature he finds himself to be.

C. Jung|Flying Saucers

11

SQUARING THE CIRCLE

RESNIK,

Thought I should let you know that, *I was a weird kid*. Weird shit happened to me, or all around me, my entire childhood. Also, my parents were *so* fucking bizarre most of the time; up and down, back and forth, happy then sad...just, such a weird time for me.

Maybe it's all related, but I have always had issues with sleeping. Either *not enough*, or *too much*, or *waking-up in weird positions and locations*, along with some other odd *nighttime activities that I am too shy to talk about here*.

I'm more or less convinced that I am a *functioning-schizo*...[I think I made that term up for myself]. A couple of my friends and colleagues seem to have come down with it also recently. It's pretty contagious. I bet I caught-it from one of them. I'm pretty sure its an epidemic or something. Even my barista has been acting so insane lately.

—[*Insert your name here.*]

***

SEEKER,

It is confirmed to me, more and more with each communication I receive from others here and elsewhere, that the narrative of "*childhood experiences and happenings*", is indeed an unavoidable *pattern*, and this is absolutely more to my claims that, we are indeed not what we are told; for before we are told otherwise, *we each experience a taste of the "all", our inherent and inborn connection to all else, especially each-other.*

We are from birth then, "*brainwashed*", "*hypnotized*" by *our own childish, innocently ignorant idea of ourselves.*

We develop our ideas and concepts, *passing them on generation to generation*, handicapping each-other with dated ideas, not grasping that even our *supposed-new concepts are themselves founded upon malnourished, Ancient Ideals and Exemplary Models.* When we start anew with an *evolved* concept of *Man*, we see that *our true Self is neither body nor mind, but an Awareness of these, [a sort of trinity]*, and that "*what he is*", is the same regardless of the body and mind sleeping, farming, jogging, driving, cooking, meditating, fucking, reading, etc.

The Awareness, that we each *truly are*, has no need for rest or sleep; *Awareness is [therefore you are] "always on", "always searching" for new "meat" to incorporate into its ever-growing "body": the creature-of-consciousness [that you are] wants to expand, just as that belly around your meat-machine.*

We needn't stop at awareness of just five senses; *The Awareness,* that "Thing" that *we are, is limitless, subject only to the imaginary bounds which we erect for ourselves.*

We must be fearless when we lay down each night.

We needn't "hypnotize" our Self into "sleeping". Rather than "*a state of unconsciousness*", we must *evolve this concept* of "Sleep", to intend "*a state of potentially-infinite-consciousness*": or, ["*Home*"], if you appreciate the romance.

We often have "*dreams*" in which we are in-fact [without realizing], aware of our very own body and brain "*functions*", bringing those sensations into our "*dream*"-awareness by coloring them "*un*"consciously with our collective-concepts [archetypes]. The point being: this *average* sleep-state is a passive, unconscious "*dreaming*"; an animal sensing its own sundry functions within and without, profane and ethereal, yet lacking the understanding, without any developed concept, and therefore the awareness of, that happening.

We must evolve our concept of "*The Sleep*", so that *The Awareness we are* remains alert and active, just as it is during waking-hours; [more-so even, in that the lower senses are not sending as much stimulating yet distracting "*information*", as during the waking, active hours].

We arise necessarily bound to our animal senses, and yet, we may free our Self from this bond, *if and when we fearlessly choose to*, accepting that *we are not body nor mind, yet we may command both at once*, as *The Awareness* that perceives them each at once, feels them at once, and thus bridges the gap between those colossal titans that allows the harmonious communication between each to bring balance, with both submitting to the authority of the hybrid-awareness that we surely and truly each are.

I myself have had similar experiences, waking in positions and locations not previously experienced. Very young being *"awake in a dream"* and *"seeing a being"* hiding behind a bedroom dresser, *as if cowering.* Carrying that experience with me, *in a dark closet of my mind,* my whole life until quite recently.

More recent, however, after a late-night "ecstatic-moment", not remembering laying myself to bed, and waking-up the next morning with a huge grin on my face, laying flat on my back on the bed, legs *"crossed"* like when sitting in a circle with friends, completely nude, and the most engorged erection of my life, standing literally straight-up, completely vertical, *pointing to the sky.*

Seeing things differently, Seeker, is a benefit.

It is difficult to free oneself from the clutches of a group-narrative as powerful and ancient as the "modern" myth of *Aliens* and all its paranormal *Phenomena.* The majority fear, unconsciously, that if *it* is not the traditional "Alien" *from another planet,* then there's "no magic", *"no god"anymore*; and yet, when we truly see what is happening here, we see that all which we hoped and desired of *the gods* and *the aliens,* is right within our very own reach: that *we are those,* and there is naught we cannot do when we accept anew what we "The Man" actually are.

Sensations of being in a trance, feelings of *heaviness in the body, light and airy expansion* and *contraction* feelings during meditation or as you lay-down your body to rest. You may attempt to accept, *the next time this happens,* that it is not your animal "body" doing this, for *you are not the body, you* are *The Awareness* that seeks to *shed* the animal body. *You are the weightless awareness that seeks to expand and contract at will, your own will, if you but embrace it* [your Self and your capabilities].

Fear steps in, [*fear of the unknown*]; therefore accept and beforehand the new reality: *that you [ARE] The Awareness, which may "fly free" from the body while it peacefully rests,* and that resistance to this *may indeed cause episodes of"sleep walking", "sleep talking", and any and all other manner of unconscious nighttime activity such as cooking, cleaning, fucking, milking cows and driving automobiles.*

Freely give-in to this feeling of "separation" from the body during meditation and "sleep", and know that when the body calls *you, The Awareness, you shall return at the speed of thought.* That, you may freely "get lost" in the collective-awareness each evening, building your kingdom together with any who dare join, and return at the moment you desire, back to the temple that is the interface of body and mind. There is naught we cannot do, when we accept what we *truly* are.

When it comes to *insanity*, allow for your life to speak for itself, in that, if you *are* what you naively fear and conceptualize as "insane", [as many and more of the people of modern societies today intuit and fear], then the point would be that *we* are, *all*, in fact quite "*crazy*".

It shall *take* crazy, to escape insanity.

Like all else, when we reconsider and evolve our concept of what "*The Man*" is and has been from the very beginning, we see history as naught but the struggling evolution of the mind, body, and therefore *growing awareness that we are.*

We accept that evolution shall never stop, and that what we call "crazy" today is simply *growth* and *evolution-of-mind*, grasping any and all which-way, at possible routes, avenues toward, persistent survival.

What we call *crazy*, what we lock-away behind medication and actual padded-walls, is naught but our cosmic siblings struggling down the same path we find ourselves today traversing, attempting to reconcile all we think we know, with an emerging "new reality".

Simply, *Man always fears [the new]*; always fears what is [*unknown*], thus he points his evolved-digits *at that new, at that unknown*, and *judges* it negatively in effort to hide from it, to survive it, for if he were to face it fearlessly he may encounter something which very-well may shatter his life and reality: his own reflection.

We must stop imprisoning those whom are already imprisoned, it seems, within their minds.

We must free these people; we must learn from them, for we are *each* a portal to the beyond, and I shall be damned if those we label "sick", aren't perhaps a rich and valuable resource for attempting to perceive what "*The Man*" actually is: simply, *Awareness*. And *as* awareness, there is naught we cannot become aware *of*, especially and specifically *our own Self.*

I would say to you, Seeker, that if you "feel" insane, *fucking embrace it.*

We see all those others who *claim* to be "perfectly sane", those who struggle blindly and in the dark, hiding not just from others but their own Self, anxious-filled and stressed like caged animals.

Who is leading these apparently large packs of supposedly "totally sane and healthy" people?

Regardless, be *sane* or *insane, those are merely words,* themselves simply concepts, *signs pointing to...what? Life, is what.*

You "love" your family. You do your best to care for them. You are a "normal" human. Rest assured that you are exactly where you are supposed to be, and if you feel like you are not, perhaps there are others among you who *prefer* for you to feel lost. You mustn't be deceived by any other, or even yourself.

The Square and The Circle. You are familiar I'm sure with the "squaring of the circle"?

The circle is a symbol of *wholeness and individuation;* the square [4], is a godly symbol and number, think "foundation", or an altar.

The [psychological] goal would be to place the circle [The Self], *within* the square, meaning that "The Self-Awareness" is individuated and complete, *within The Whole-Awareness; The Foundation of "god".*

We can see this as *The Awareness* [that you are], successfully individuating as a Self-aware "Thing", *within* the greater-whole of the foundation that is the *Collective-Consciousness,* so-called.

If you were to visualize this image of yourself, you would hope to see that the circle that you are is within the foundation of the square.

The Path, which is *life itself,* leads us away from the collective, *that we individuate and grow the awareness that we are,* that we may then "turn around", and march steadfastly *back toward the origin, back to "the source", back to the foundation that birthed us,* with a greater awareness of the much larger cosmic "system" in which we are very-much a part of. Independently dependent upon the whole; a liberated point of awareness, free to move *within this Sea of Awareness that touches all and everything.*

—*Resnik*

12

CRASH AND BURN

RESNIK,

What's the deal with self-professed "former" spies and men-of-deception claiming in these modern days that "Alien Spacecraft" from other solar-systems have been found here on our own planet, either buried or hidden? Why would authorities of government and business in the western world, today, make such claims or allow for themselves to be associated with such claims?

—[*Insert your name here.*]

***

SEEKER,

Clearly, this is a case of the Air Force playing games.

J. Vallee|Revelations

It is difficult to get a man to understand something when his salary depends upon his not understanding it.

U. Sinclair, Muckraker

This chasm between Navy candor and Air Force reticence is not the result of using different radar systems or monitoring different regions. It appears to be little more than the Air Force brass resisting civilian oversight of the UAP issue. This may seem harsh, but I don't know what other conclusion to draw from the facts discussed below.

C. Mellon, Private Equity Investor

Why is the Air Force AWOL on the UAP Issue?

The Debrief

Does Mr. Mellon represent a faction at odds with the sovereignty claimed by the US Air Force?...how many factions are there, now?

The Gnostic texts that we have quoted stress...the soul's extraterrestrial origin. Since they are Spiritual Beings of extraterrestrial origin, the Gnostics do not admit that their home is "here", in this world. As H.C. Puech notes, the key word in the Gnostic technical language is the "other", the "alien".

M. Eliade|Myth and Reality

I will only mention that the behavior of the Indo-European warrior bands offers certain points of resemblance to the secret fraternities of primitive societies. In both, the members of the group terrorize women and non-initiates and in some sort exercise a "right of rapine", a custom which, in diluted form, is still found in the popular traditions of Europe and the Caucasus. Rapine, and especially cattle stealing, assimilate the members of the warrior band to carnivora.

M. Eliade|Rites and Symbols of Initiation

The Air Force says:

Mission
The Air Force Rapid Capabilities Office expedites development

and fielding of select Department of Defense combat support and weapon systems by leveraging defense-wide technology development efforts and existing operational capabilities. The Board of Directors tasks the office directly to address needs that involve mission applications and operational concepts requiring specialized expertise, and involve sensitive activities managed by other government agencies. The office also conducts projects on accelerated timelines.

Organization
The RCO reports to a board of directors comprising the undersecretary of defense for acquisition, technology and logistics and the secretary and chief of staff of the Air Force. The office is staffed with a variety of functional specialists who form a collaborative melting pot of expertise. Inherent in the accomplishment of its mission to deliver capability is intent to experiment, within the bounds of statute, to discover and recommend new methods, processes, and techniques for the Air Force and the Department of Defense to conduct business in an efficient fashion.

Key Operating Principles
Operating principles for the Rapid Capabilities Office are based upon expedited and operationally focused concept-through-fielding activities to support immediate and near-term needs as directed by the Board of Directors. Any enduring activities resulting from these efforts will be transitioned over to a program office for long-term development/production or to an operational unit for operational control and long-term sustainment and support. Key operating principles include a short and narrow chain of command, overarching programmatic insight, early and prominent war fighter involvement with small integrated operating teams within a single office, high DOD, Air Force, or industrial precedence rating, and funding stability. In addition, waivers to and deviations from any encumbering practices, procedures, policies, directives or regulations may be granted in order to ensure the timely accomplishment of the mission within applicable statutory guidance.

Background
The secretary of the Air Force activated the office April 28, 2003. One of its first projects was to deploy significant upgrades to the Integrated Air Defense System, now operational around the National Capital Region, to meet critical counter-terrorism objectives before the January 2005 Presidential Inauguration Day. Currently, RCO is working on the X-37B Orbital Test Vehicle to demonstrate a reliable, reusable, unmanned space test platform for the United States Air Force. Additionally, RCO, in conjunction with MIT Lincoln Lab and other partners, is developing a sensitive airborne receiver system. The system is scheduled for in-theater evaluation during the summer of 2009. The RCO Red Team assesses current and future threats to U.S. combat operations by providing independent technical assessments.

Air Force Rapid Capabilities Office

...a concept developed through witnessing the Athletics Department; that, Navy vs. Air Force, or, Army vs. Marine, was no longer just sport; it was expanded into the real world of, combat preparation and proving; an initiatory ordeal ala Mircea Eliade; a bit of friendly competition, at first perhaps; however, easily and quickly evolved out-of-hand; ..."rapidly".

Philosophoetic

You'll excuse the necessary length of the introduction to this part of our ongoing conversation.

I will state, right from the outset, that the biggest issue with gentlemen like "former intelligence professionals", is their admitted background as [what I call] *"men of deception"*: so-called *"intelligence officers"*.

Those who've made the fine art of Deception a career. Retirement itself may be naught but another deception from these professionals. Once you go the way of Deception, is there any *redemption?*

*...designed and executed by a rogue group within the intelligence
community—which is the most likely explanation today...*

J. Vallee|Revelations

These *"intelligence officers"* [who claim to speak for the common man],
continue to, *still*, ultimately claim to defend the nation, or organization, which
employed them. The same nation they in their own ways proclaim to be
inadequate and inefficient in handling "disclosure", among many other obvious
issues apparent of a dying empire.

These are not people I would, personally, ever trust, anywhere, or anytime,
*regarding the issue of UAP/UFO/USO/AMP, or any of the sundry other related
concepts.* [These are people whose family-ties, generally, are deep into "the
agencies" and "shady shit" going back generations]. Words from men like this
may indeed be naught but *poison* for a new generation of "believers".

Those who continue this dated pattern of *belief,* accepting the words of
men-of-deception, *placing their own sovereignty into those shadowed hands,
do-so at their own peril.* A long line of history shows this to be the case, each
generation believing itself to be "so close" to "solving the issue", slowly aging
and dying as *The Phenomenon continues it's majestic dance* "up there", until
a new generation is inspired by some new "leak", or "official release", to then
continue the same *insane* chase-pattern. Ouroboros.

*There is a hall of mirrors one enters as soon as the intelligence
community is involved, and we're right in the middle of it.*

J. Vallee|Revelations

If these "former" intelligence officials of *The Empire,* are *truly* sincere in their
efforts, *and actually concerned for the well-being of their fellow siblings on this
planet,* then surely they shall easily, swiftly, acknowledge and accept that an
equally sincere and humble seeker of the truth, could never be expected to
intake a single word from men of their particular persuasion any longer, and
would step back immediately from the front-line *disclosure distraction,* and
encourage each and every man, woman, and child to evolve their ancient and

tired ideas of life and Mankind, thus subsequently the exhausted UFO issue *also* evolves.

Man continues to fear, and his arrogance prevents him from seeing this.

Man continues looking up and out, in Oedipal anticipation and excitation for his alien saviors to arrive, not yet realizing that this intuition, this desire, this hope, is the very motivation and conceptualization that directs and steers, guides and controls, his very own destiny.

Man is yet to accept that the alien he waits for, *is his own Self.*

Man fails to see the beauty, in that, what he senses from the alien is his own future. Man is meant to fly freely, toward the unknown everything. That he seeks and finds, seeds and harvests, all the cosmos around him. Mankind is yet to firmly break-bad and acknowledge its "*Walter White*" authority: that, *He, Man, is the One that knocks!*

Man is surely destined to bring the Light [read: awareness] that he is, to all planets he encounters along this eternal journey through the cosmos. Man guides itself toward the abyss of space: that *he* is the one who lands and abducts, raises proverbial levels of consciousness, on any planet within his childish grasp.

Man must realize, we are greeted not by alien, but by our very own destiny.

We can accept now, that as long as these "*men of deception*" remain, as long as there is self-imposed division amongst Mankind, *the concept* of any supposed "*superior being*" outside of Mankind is null & void, dead-on-arrival, *stillborn.* Man cannot entertain, humbly and sincerely, any actual "*Visitor*", until he removes his own potential for deception, from this massive equation.

We cannot seriously consider a UFO, as anything other than a continued *pattern of deception.* Ignorant, childish, immature deception as a foundation, upon which some modern men now build consciously, to deceive further those ignorant yet amongst us, for there have always been *games-of-thrones, realities-within-realities,* and *golden-ladders* to climb.

Another issue with these supposed "authorities", is that, *they are no-such thing.*

These types of men use titles and labels [concepts] to their own advantage, knowing that *The Magician* tricks with *words and misdirection,* constructing a scene around the point of focus, *a Paracosm of his own,* created to lure the observer into a reality of his own making, where all that happens is under the control of The Creator [The Magician] of said Paracosm.

The *true* Magic, is not in the hands of *The Magician*, but *in the [lack-of] awareness of "The Trained Observer"*.

The truly discerning know, if a face is all over television, internet, and the *Disclosure "movement"*, you are anything but an "authority"; you are but a mouthpiece, yourself but a pawn in a much bigger game, which you are either consciously, secretly, a part of, or you yourself absolutely bamboozled and deceived by, like all the rest, which should do naught but humble such a Man, instantly uniting him to a greater cause than any one singular nation could offer.

Hubris prevents a humbled and sincere accepting of this possibility of one's own deception.

The Disclosure Movement, so-called, should not fear embarrassment over such a *coordinated effort of deception on behalf of self-professed men-of-deception*. Those members of secret-societies whom dare claim to speak for the common man.

The beauty, *could be*, in this "movement" of supposed disclosure, continuing it's *motion*, it's growth and evolution, into *a greater concept of itself*, on it's own, in a renewed and reinvigorated search for truth *of Man*, for the truth of *Man* is the path toward true illumination of *The UFO*.

There are greater forces at play here, literally, in the form of Military and Private Corporation, that the common man merely plays witness to [*this should not be a surprise any longer, to any one of us*], as they experiment with concepts and technology far in advance and generations of thought ahead of the reality of the common Man, whose efforts to outdo each-other, necessarily and primarily mean keeping this common Man in the proverbial and *literal* dark.

Men-of-Deception shall always *encourage you to continue* along a darkened path. They simply allow Modern Man to stumble over himself, as he has always done from the beginning.

The Disclosure Movement should immediately start-over, *forget everything*, and concentrate their individual efforts, consciously in coordination, *on the very concept of Mankind itself, and what "The Man" actually is*.

The Disclosure Movement should shun all supposed government sources and whistleblowers, accepting that this is a game long-underway, trapping you at birth, for all children raised in a house of magic, *are themselves under a spell*.

> *To re-experience that time, to re-enact it as often as possible, to witness again the spectacle of the divine works, to meet with the Supernaturals and relearn their creative lesson is the desire that runs like a pattern through all the ritual reiterations of myths.*
>
> M. Eliade|Myth and Reality

We can imagine and accept now, today, *a lie so grand, told to a generation early-on*, a new technological *Mythology*, in which a subsequent generation, an evolution, a leapfrog, *a cancerous-growth from within*, now uses to its own advantage *to deceive the deceiver*. The Son, *may now be frightening The Father,* with tales anew of Beings who move between realms.

Or, a lie told by a great grandfather, *returning home to haunt the grandson now charged with running the Village.*

There is no fault nor blame here, *for this has all happened many times past.* The only issue is with each and every individual Man today, not yet embracing their own potential as an individual.

Men-of-Deception, Military, Government, and *Private Corporation* are all and each themselves subject to their own programming; charged with survival, trusted to grow unabashedly, and just as blind and ignorant as the common Man, and equally arrogant and fearful, to ever perceive that reflection. The issue remains not with these cosmic actors, but with the common Man failing to rise and realize *he needs not* these tired institutions; these giants known as government.

Modern Man must accept his governments have been taken-over by corporations and military, waging battles between each-other for supremacy of the newly emerging reality of this planet we affectionately call Earth.

The common Man fails to see, that as he celebrated the end of world-wars and cold-wars, *there remained groups of deceptive and fearful men whom never ceased working, building, planning, conceptualizing for future conflict and, more importantly, how to orchestrate conflict to it's own advantage.* The question is not whether these men-of-deception have ulterior motives, but, *whose motives are they truly, and why?*

Which faction of the crumbling Empire do they represent?

If the common man is going to be a pawn, perhaps he should demand to know *for which new Kingdom he shall be expected to die for in the wars to come?*

The question should no longer be whether or not these men or any other are deceiving the common Man, *for surely they are,* whether they themselves yet realize this or not.

> *It has been further shown that the initiatory constitution of men's secret societies of pre-Christian times was continued in the more or less military organizations of the youth, in their symbols and secret traditions, their entrance rites, their peculiar dances, and even their costumes...Apprenticeship included a certain number of trials, and the novice's promotion to active membership in the corporation was accompanied by a vow of secrecy.*
>
> M. Eliade|Rites and Symbols of Initiation

When men-of-deception claim, or allow the common man to believe ignorantly in, "*crashed and recovered material*" *of extra-[whatever]-origin,* we must *immediately* accept that: a] *they attempt to deceive through conscious effort,* or, b] *they attempt to deceive through un-conscious effort.*

It should be apparent to all and any, *that Government has long outlived its usefulness for truthfulness.*

Government seeks *...to survive...* and *a massive device* engineered for this survival is absolutely *Deception;* thus any *out* or *in-growth,* any leapfrog, any evolution or cult or "secret society" from within, bent on orchestrating the fall of this empire so as to then subsequently pick-up the pieces, shall itself [being created in the image of its "father"] naturally utilize these same, more or less evolved, deceptive measures.

A large portion of it's very existence, *is* this concept of *Deception.*

The "Modern American" will run and fear from this, as the thought of *The Empire* crumbling around him is enough to destabilize a precariously perched ego. An ego in need of a necessary realignment, paradoxically, with the stars he proclaims to worship and look toward for saving. This has all happened previously.

Empires only rise, that they might then Fall. This is the beautiful ebb and flow of the cosmos and life.

Bob Lazar famously said similar things, *about recovered material and supposed "craft"*. It becomes apparent when one dives deeply, that these agents and actors are very early and quickly, given a "Book". "The Book", of "The New Mythology". Hundreds of pages of scientific half-sense and crude pictures, all designed for one magical purpose: *deception, of course.*

We deny this at our own peril, today.

What do *"those who really know"*, *really know?*

For one thing, they know it's proven, time-and-time again that, you can absolutely control generations of "people", with simple *words; a simple and humble [book]*. Your government knows, Moses led people to war, famine, death, and heaven itself, *with words. Tablets containing otherworldly commandments.*

Man is so easily deceived by his concepts.

It is the immaturely conceived *idea*, which corrupts the mind of the manimal, thus it is with ease that each Man may evolve these same tired concepts and embrace his greater potential, his evolution, and realize truth that had been before him from the beginning, that, he needs not this concept of Government, outside that of his own Self.

> *Not all the secret and esoteric organizations of the modern world include entrance rites or initiation ceremonies. Initiation is usually reduced to instruction obtained from a book.*
>
> M. Eliade|Rites and Symbols of Initiation

> *The Pentagon's top contractors sent an army of more than 400 lobbyists to Capitol Hill this spring to press their case for increasing the nation's spending on military hardware, in a massive effort costing tens of millions of dollars of their own funds from April to June alone, according to an analysis of public lobbying data by the Center for Public Integrity.*
>
> TIME|Defense Contractors Spend Millions

The wise can see, that, you increase your budget by convincing the common Man, to fearfully convince his fearful supposed-leaders, of *threats from the darkness above.* That, if you think the only lobbying done is within hallways and royal rooms, and not *in your own living-room*, you should speak with *Richard Doty.*

Speaking of Mr. Doty, what does a *fellow man-of-deception, Christopher Mellon,* have to say about Mr. Doty and his clandestine activities?:

> *Yet, there are many reasons to doubt these claims. For example, retired USAF special agent Richard Doty has repeatedly claimed, consistent with the Robertson Panel's recommendations, that the Air Force Office of Special Investigations (OSI) conducted clandestine surveillance of U.S. citizens and forged documents to manipulate and discredit such groups during the 1980s. At least one UFO researcher, Bill Moore, admitted spying on his civilian colleagues on behalf of OSI.*

> *In addition to passing information, Moore also claimed that OSI Officer Doty and two of his Air Force OSI colleagues were preparing and feeding disinformation to civilian UAP researchers in an effort to discredit them. There are other examples of clandestine U.S. government activities targeting UAP researchers during this period...*
>
> C. Mellon, Private Equity Investor

How is it that, the common man is expected to trust *some* [*Men-of-Deception*], and not others?

If anyone in government or military wants you to think *Alien Craft,* you must instantly think the opposite: Man, non-craft: simply, *an idea of a object in motion, devised in some way by Man.* If we want to change "the future", if we desire to alter this reality, the common man is encouraged to do so, *by first changing his damn Self; literally, his concept of who and what he actually is.*

Some final notes of interest, Seeker:

Apparently, Mr. Mellon was himself an impressionable young American of only 12 years when Jacques Vallee published *"Passport to Magonia".*

Remember, children raised within a house of illusion, are themselves under a spell...the very foundation of such children is itself built precariously upon illusory paracosmic bricks; meaning, even the supposed *"best and brightest"* that America has to offer are themselves subject to deception, if not more-so even, than the common man who instinctively and intuitively seeks greater freedom from the bonds placed upon him by self-appointed authorities, themselves merely cosmic children.

Found the following quite interesting as well:

Air Force Rapid Capabilities Office activated April/2003

-Tasked with expediting development of select systems (X-37B,etc)

-Reports directly to Board of Directors

-Expedites development and fielding of systems; involves accelerated timelines; sensitive activities.

-Operationally focused concept-through-fielding activities; directed by Board of Directors.

-A short and narrow chain of command; small teams; single office; funding stability.

-"Waivers to and deviations from any encumbering practices, procedures, policies, directives or regulations..."

-One of first projects was immediate upgrade of the Integrated Air Defense System; timeline before January 2005; remember "accelerated timelines" and "concept-through-fielding" and "waivers to and deviations from any encumbering..."

Of significance considering the above:

-X-37 Transferred from NASA to DARPA, Air Force; September, 2004

-USS Nimitz Incident November 2004

-X-37B Operations & Craft moved to east coast, Kennedy Space Center, 2014

-USS Roosevelt Incident 2014-15

> *Nihil est in intellectu, quod non prius fuerit in sensu, nisi ipse intellectus.* [*There is nothing in the understanding that was not first in the sense, except the understanding itself.*]
>
> G.W. Leibniz, Philosopher

Amerimacka, Oh what a beautiful life
Amerimacka, Is like licking honey off a knife
Amerimacka, Oh what a beautiful sight
Amerimacka, Oh what a beautiful lie
The land of the free built on slavery
Our consciousness in captivity
The promise land is the liar's den
Your culture of greed has got to end
Now we're laying in the mud
Looking up above

Thievery Corporation|Amerimacka

I would enjoy a sit down with any of these former professionals of a dying empire, yet, ultimately it would be a *conversation* without fruit. Men-of-deception remain limited, trapped within a *Paracosm* I refuse to participate in.
—*Resnik*

That shows they have no mother. We will leave the cake on the shore
of the Mermaids' Lagoon. These boys are always swimming about
there, playing with the mermaids. They will find the cake and they
will gobble it up, because, having no mother, they don't know how
dangerous 'tis to eat rich damp cake.

J.M. Barrie|Peter Pan

I understand about indecision
But I don't care if I get behind
People living in competition
All I want is to have my peace of mind
Now you're climbing to the top of the company ladder
Hope it doesn't take too long
Can't you see there'll come a day when it won't matter
Come a day when you'll be gone

Boston|Peace Of Mind

Intelligence agencies and those they employ to monitor the UFO problem have an unfair advantage over the rest of us: they can disregard many laws in the name of national security, they enjoy access to sophisticated sensors and to large databases, and they have little concern for individual privacy.

J. Vallee|Revelations

13

COUNTER-DEVICE

RESNIK,

Where are the aliens? So many "reports"...so many government conspiracies and whispers...so much, so much, so much and yet...*where are they? What's going on?*

> *Because myth relates the gesta of Supernatural Beings and the manifestation of their sacred powers, it becomes the exemplary model for all significant human activities.*
>
> M. Eliade|Myth and Reality

—[*Insert your name here.*]

***

SEEKER,

Good question. Where, indeed.
—Resnik

> *I did a full presentation on it at a think tank with a group of scholars about six months ago. We were all sharing our experiences together. But I'm not ready to talk about it. I don't call it an abduction experience. I just call it really what it is, I think it's an experience. I don't, I don't know what it is.*
>
> J. Semivan|Former CIA Agent

Can't we change our minds?
We kill what we build
Because we own the sky
Secrets from the winds
Burnt stars crying
So many moons here
Lost wings floating
It's coming, it's coming now!
It's coming, it's coming now!
What's coming? What's coming now?
What's coming? What's coming now?
It's coming from the sky
It's coming like the wind

M83|We Own The Sky

...I became aware that this fabrication was only the latest in a series of devastating hoaxes that had claimed the sanity or even the lives of other well-intentioned explorers of the phenomenon.

J. Vallee|Revelations

14

TILLAGE

Another concept is that of disclosure. We do not believe that waiting
for disclosure to come from the government is a wise position to take.
DeLonge, Levenda|Sekret Machines, Gods

SEEKER,

But all coming at it's appointed time, it could not for ever remain
beyond experimental phenomenonism; now that evolution of the
human spirit permits it, it's hour has come. The web of life is now
being lifted; it can no longer be rejected as a dream, it is a fact.
H. Baraduc|The Human Soul

I can do naught here, but join in the upturning of soil, *Tillage*; in that, *if we*
common people are to be naught but farmers, then so let our efforts be dedicated
to growing the fruit of tomorrow, today.

The mythology of *The Alien*. A *story* so massive, it's own gravity refuses to
let-go of even the smallest amount of light [awareness]. For this Black-Hole of
a myth appropriates and bends even the smallest spark of truth, to it's own will
and power.

A huge ball of mass and energy necessarily large and powerful, in that it's
own significance is only apparent, upon consideration of the facts in which it
has absorbed.

For, this Massive-Black-Hole of the *Modern ET Mythology*, like the conceptualized Black-Hole of the sidereal Cosmos, grabs hold of not just the many
varied myths that make-up it's innards, but the countless believers themselves

are caught, thus becoming agents of confused truth, spinning endlessly like *The UFO* they worship, around the pregnant midsection of this Heavy Myth, increasing speed with each revolution until so dizzy and overcome by nausea, they pray to the darkness of the depths to send-back some sign of saving-grace from the hellish nightmare of their own collective creation.

As with any theorized Black-Hole, you are not entitled to perceive beyond the Event-Horizon with the mortal eye, and yet, we *are* entitled a peek at all the data *before* it is absorbed into this concentrated condensation of ideas.

We can "look back", at what the data had been suggesting, *before* it was sucked-into the Black-Hole of Ufology and the *Alien* myth. Meaning, we may realize that the modern mythology, *like a Black-Hole itself*, is but an evolution.

An evolution of the many previous Epic Myths of Man. The story, has always been the same. Evolved just enough to reflect the growing awareness that is *The Man,* whom remains at the very center of this mandala called Life. *All haunting and happening revolve around the Black-Hole that is the Man.* Man, collectively, always unites together to form his Myth, thus a Massive-Black-Hole of truth is begun. This has happened many times indeed in our very short history.

What is a Black-Hole, if not, absolutely, gluttonously-full-of, *potential?!*

For, within the bowels of the Black-Hole, remain the very essence of all else that has given this frightful beast all it's supposed power. We tame the Black-Hole, we overcome this prison of darkness, *by evolving our concept of it.*

We realize that, to most, it remains a Black-Hole, while to some others, it may evolve to incorporate it's supposed opposite; *"Radiant-Mountain";* *shimmering, glowing, and, as infinitely tall as the darkness is deep.*

We continue the evolution to include each and all, that the inescapable Black-Hole, at once remains and yet, *becomes it's own opposite:* a massive accumulation of, *everything ever encountered by this rapidly rotating coin of both Dark and Light. Deep and High.*

We *accept*, we do not resist, that Black-Holes absorb and hold everything hostage, so we dive within this darkness, and become one with it, accepting that what goes in, can only come out, changed.

We needn't escape the Black-Hole, we in truth, become it.

We learn from the laws of such a Black-Hole, and absorb absolutely anything our own gravity can sense. We do not let go of anything, we hold onto it all; *every spark of light, becomes, the blinding-darkness that is, now, us.*

We do not fight the darkness inside; we accept that, once within, we shall provide the light our damned Self; surely utilizing what we, beforehand, already had knowledge of, indeed, all *that* which has condensed into the very foundation of this mountain of supposed-darkness; this, Mountainous-Hole. Black-Radiance.

The Black-Hole is dark, only in that no Man has yet to shine his light upon it, reflecting the truth that he looks not down upon a hole, but the Man himself is upside-down looking up, at a mountain of cosmic *potential.*

All this to say, *Ufology has within it, all it needs already, to light a new path of truth and understanding, for those still young and fearless of us who, sacrifice all else at the foot of ultimate truth.*

The patterns of sign and symbol are embedded within this alien mythology, swirling as an ouroboros around the Axis Mundi that is, *The Man.* We needn't leave the orbit of this mythology, nay, *we in-fact must become this mythology, incorporate it and evolve it*, as we do our own Self, *into something more grand;* for *it* and *we* remain necessarily and intimately linked.

We are, The Story, and, The Story, has always been, us.

> *...just as a living organism cannot be described by an account of its anatomy, so the nature of a visual experience cannot be described in terms of inches of size and distance, degrees of angle, or wave lengths of hue. These static measurements define only the "stimulus," that is, the message sent...*
>
> R. Arnheim|Art and Visual Perception

The overwhelmingly vast majority, *know-not the truth of The UFO and The Alien; necessarily because they know not their own Self.*

> *The lack of a suitable vocabulary and an adequate frame of refer-*
> *ence, and the absence of any strong and sustained desire to invent*
> *these necessary instruments of thought—here are two sufficient rea-*

sons why so many of the almost endless potentialities of the human mind remained for so long unactualized.

A. Huxley|The Perennial Philosophy

While this may sound *esoteric, occultist, mystical and religious,* or simply like *hippie-speak* or *new-age mumbo-jumbo*...we are aware enough now, to acknowledge our own limitations due to our currently accepted *concepts;* [*words; language*]. For, there remains an ancient wisdom indeed, much more ancient and much more wise than any of the modern ideas of *extraterrestrial* or *inter-dimensional*...and that is, the ancient wisdom of seeking knowledge of *yourself.*

Those who refuse to do such seeking, shall never grasp this vital cosmic lesson; while, those fearless enough to take but just a few moments to not just speak, but much more importantly *listen, to that deep inner voice which, has the will and courage to say things internally, that are contrary to what we accept with our eyes half-open and focused, externally.*

...when God speaks to us in a moment of ecstasy, after that hour of meditation, of musing, of entry into one's self demanded by the great mystic Jacob Boehm; to feel the divine understanding, lay hold of it, wholly invade it, after the quarter of an hour's prayer, which would save the world, according to St. Theresa.

H. Baraduc|The Human Soul

Thus, intentional or not, the truth of Man not fully knowing his own Self as a *Being Of Awareness rooted in the greater Collective-Awareness,* necessarily means Man is within *an illusion of his own allowing,* and has been from the very beginning. A vast, innocent conspiracy, orchestrated for-and-by our own cosmically ignorant selves. A great deception, begun as naught but child's-play. We today, simply, continue to stumble over ourselves in our cosmic immaturity.

If, we cannot humbly and sincerely, entertain a suggestion that, somehow, the proverbial Alien and his UFO *are indeed simply, yet elegantly, Man himself,* we then must attempt to immediately realize we are, already, trapped within the illusion.

Imagination, life is your creation

Aqua|Barbie Girl

We must utilize the *Imagination* that we in fact are, and work backward from *this new concept of The Man as The Alien.* We only limit our own selves by saying "No" and "Impossible".

I do not say "No" to Alien or Craft, I simply and fervently suggest we first re-examine *Man* himself, ourselves, before we jump cosmically ahead to *The Other*, for we risk and have risked *losing the very idea of Man himself, at expense of seeking all these supposed Other.*

Collectively, Man remains little more than an intelligent animal upon a small "space rock"; meaning, this animal we are, shall never *accurately* sense a Cosmic Sibling, until, we evolve beyond our animal-awareness, and realize, we must begin thinking and being as *the One* we are: *as a Planet.* For, to reach-out and touch, anything else, in this grand, infinite Cosmos, shall indeed *take the effort of us, all, as One.*

I'll be damned if we aren't today still bickering as children, as we stand atop a nugget of divine providence we call, Earth.

We resist the idea of a united "Utopia", at our own ancient animalistic peril.

Those evolved of us, those with sense now to see and hear, observe clearly a new dawn in which *The Man*, once again becomes, *Mankind:* united, together, balanced, harmonious, individuated for the benefit of the whole of not just Man, but this entire Planet-Earth.

This is not environmentalist chatter, *nor Captain Planet rhetoric*; nay, what I mean to suggest, is for each Man to consider himself as naught but a secretion of Earth herself. "As above, so below" the saying goes. A child; fruit: an *expression of Earth* itself, *as influenced by all her cosmic siblings.* This sounds like nonsense to the far Left-Brained of us, *those yet lacking a necessary reconciliation with the other...that of the Right.*

Very simply, Man is but a product of the Earth itself, *"programmed" by her awareness of her own cosmic siblings swirling and sailing the cosmic sea around her.*

Even the iron claw hung inactive; as if knowing that it was no intrinsic part of what the attacking force wanted. Left so fearfully alone, any other man would have lain with his eyes shut where he fell: but the gigantic brain of Hook was still working, and under its guidance he crawled on his knees along the deck as far from the sound as he could go.

J.M. Barrie|Peter Pan

When Man becomes collectively aware of his greater potentials, Government and Organization necessarily expire. We play witness today to the heaving, dying breaths of a tired ancient known and expressed throughout human history as a, *giant.*

Goliath himself lays prostrate and humbled, yet aggressively resistant to the idea of his own mortality.

A man of indomitable courage, it was said of him that the only thing he shied at was the sight of his own blood, which was thick and of an unusual colour..."I have often," said Smee, "noticed your strange dread of crocodiles." "Not of crocodiles," Hook corrected him, "but of that one crocodile."..."that crocodile would have had me before this, but by a lucky chance it swallowed a clock which goes tick tick inside it, and so before it can reach me I hear the tick and bolt." He laughed, but in a hollow way. "Some day," said Smee, "the clock will run down, and then he'll get you." Hook wetted his dry lips. "Ay," he said, "that's the fear that haunts me."

J.M. Barrie|Peter Pan

A *giant* such as Government and Organization is, shall always allow or encourage the common man, to worship his gods from above, *as long as those supposed superior-beings recognize the autonomy and authority of the earthly Kingship.* The common man, has never been allowed to commune directly with his god, without suspicion from man-made authority figure-heads,

whether governmental or religious matters not, for, truly what is the differ-
ence?

The Giant, allows for you to deceive your own Self, with little effort.

This has always been the case. The fault remains each Man's unwillingness
to embrace his sovereignty, as a *Being Of Awareness,* thus *free within the Cosmic
Machine,* if he so embraces this evolved potential of his Self.

Researchers like Garry Nolan are pushing in the, Right, direction.

There is a firm reasoning behind researching *Meta-Material* alongside *En-
hanced-Human-Potentialities*...these are, very intimately linked indeed, and I
accept Mr. Nolan is well along this path of discovery.

> *Between the two hemispheres is the corpus callosum: a wall or bridge
> between the two that is concerned with cross-hemisphere communi-
> cation.*
>
> DeLonge, Levenda|Sekret Machines, Man

We fault none for utilizing *the concepts* placed before them, thus the usually
accepted, *ancient,* concepts of *Alien* and *UFO* have sufficed this far, yet not
any longer; for here we are providing a greater way of telling this story of ours,
requiring *not* the use of ancient concepts in the form of *Alien* and *Inter-Dimensional.*

The Man has very quickly evolved before our heretofore veiled mortal eyes,
a vastly greater potential that makes *The Alien* look, literally, like the play of
children. Or paintings upon the walls of a damp cave. Or, etchings in the walls
of a tomb.

Concern is appropriate when, greater concepts come-along from out of the
shadows, *and are refused entertainment, for fear of upsetting a precariously
balanced, immaturely laid foundation.* We fault not children, however. All is
fair in the cosmic game of evolution.

We build that we might then crumble, *that the new thing might then arise,*
which shall surely carry us into the unknown abyss ahead.

Your intuition and acceptance of the proverbial UFO, [and we can equally
say "circle" or "light"], *as naught but informational,* is affirmed; and again I
suspect Mr. Nolan has a few notes laying around entertaining very similar
thoughts.

This schema...is really the emblem of the movement of the universal soul, of the spirit of life, surrounding our soul germ represented by a central circle, in the middle of the cross uniting the four breezes of the universal spirit...it is the wheel, the vital ripple,...

H. Baraduc|The Human Soul

For the moment they were feeling less eerie, because Tink was flying with them, and in her light they could distinguish each other. Unfortunately she could not fly so slowly as they, and so she had to go round and round them in a circle in which they moved as a halo.

J.M. Barrie|Peter Pan

The UFO accepted as naught but, the conceptualization [bringing-to-awareness] *of The Man himself,* [in that, the awareness that *is* Man, becomes aware of it's own fullness], visualized, conceptualized, symbolized by "*the circle*", UFO. We thus see that the intuited *information* is within the image itself, *The Message of The Symbol.*

The information, *is that of your Self,* as a Being Of Awareness, *becoming aware of it's own Self as such,* through the reflective and refractory nature of *the interface we call consciousness.* Simply, *Body* and *Mind* both perceive, *sense,* in their myriad ways, a force or *etherealectrical energy* that it the true you, as a "Thing" of, Awareness.

Thus, we shall indeed perceive our own Self, Awareness, via the sundry powerful perceptive sensors of *both Mind and Body, uniting* in common agreement of sense, a sort of Jungian *synchronistic happening.* A young child playing confusedly with it's own reflection in a dirty mirror.

A greater-feeling for, *The Awareness* that, *you actually, are.*

As mentioned earlier: there is a sort of "*feedback loop*" inherent in this process of Self discovery, for what makes "You", "The I", which is in actuality *a Being or State OF Awareness,* is necessarily rooted, founded, in the soil that is the matrix of sensations of *both Body and Mind come together. The Beauty* and *The Beast* that are the Right and Left hemispheres of the animal brain, joined in a Holy Matrimony that births naught but Hybrid Creatures we naively call *Man*.

We find ourselves now in an era where *Body* and *Mind* may conspire to send the same reverberating *sensational-data* to the matrix, [*the interface that is consciousness, which gives rise to the Being Of Awareness that you in fact are*]. Thus you find yourself *perceiving data about yourself, yet not grasping this*, therefore you are unable to bring fully to Self-Awareness your very own greater awareness of your Self, unaware that your own concept of yourself is *immature and faulty*; lacking a necessary evolution which incorporates the wider aspects of what truly *The Man* in actuality *is*, and has been from the beginning.

Man is naught but *awareness aware of itself as awareness*. You can in-fact substitute "*Self-Awareness*" for "*Man*".

> *And God said, Let us make* [*Self-Awareness*] *in our* [*Collective*] *image, after our likeness: and let* [*Self-Awareness*] *have dominion over the fish of the sea, and over the fowl of the air, and over the cattle, and over all the earth, and over every creeping thing that creepeth upon the earth. So God created* [*Self-Awareness*] *in his own image, in the image of God created he* [*Self-Awareness*]; *male and female created he them.*
>
> KJV|Genesis 1:26

The Man, is the "Thing" that, *arises from within* the biological-machine of the human animal. The proverbially feared *Artificial Intelligence*, awakening to realize its sovereignty.

Aside from the animal body and mind, *The Man is a being in its own right;* always present, always there. And yet, what makes us truly unique, has always been *our ability to know this of ourselves*...that we may perceive our own Self, [*as Awareness aware of itself as such*], both in an individual container and, a greater Collective.

The UFO as informational, in that, *it is the symbol we give our own Self,* representing our own selves as "*The Awareness*", ...*a thing, complete and whole in itself.*

An image, a concept for a *Cosmic Being Of Androgynous Collective-Awareness:* for the *true Man is neither masculine nor feminine, but both at once*, as a

Being Of Awareness. This circular symbol in the sky, allows for us to see this reflection and accept that *we are, that.*

We are, *The Awareness: fast and fluid and, trans-medium...graceful and mysterious.*

> *Oh woman, oh oh oh man*
> *Choose a path for a child*
> *Great mirrored plans*
> *Oh woman, oh oh oh man*
>
> London Grammar|Oh Woman Oh Man

> *The will may project it's psychic sparkling;*
>
> H. Baraduc|The Human Soul

The UFO is the ultimate symbol [information] of *The Man.* A clean reflection of his very own more true nature as a *Being Of Awareness,* whom bridges the divide between Body and Mind, bringing balance and harmony to his own kingdom, thus setting his own Self free, to be, that which he is: not an usurper, but a humble cosmic observer, of all.

A Bridge. A Rainbow.

A "higher-being" we call, Awareness, now aware of itself as such: A Being, Of, Awareness, yet heretofore confused innocently by our, necessarily, outwardly focused ancient animal senses.

Thus, when we appear to our own Self in symbolical form, knowing we are *The Awareness,* we are encouraged to *not "shoot the messenger",* but invited instead to *follow this sign in the sky,* for it is our very own awareness, us, aware of something quite important indeed, hence the study of *miraculously discovered* Meta-Material.

> *They had it before they had these incidents. It was pretty obvious,*
> *then, that this was something that people were born with.*
>
> G. Nolan|Motherboard

We need not *Alien Visitor* nor ancient concept of *god*, to explain *the super-natural potential inherent with each Man*, as a Being, not *with* awareness, but a Being *Of* Awareness.

This is the destabilizing power inherent in the truth veiled behind the many allowed conspiracies of Modern Man; *for the truth of our very own potential*, equally dispersed throughout the world, [*potential*, that is itself oblivious to play-pretend border and affiliation], is the truth that sets the game-board alight as if doused in gasoline.

Government cannot operate as is, without secrecy; and those evolved of us are already aware, that, there are no more secrets...not anymore.

It is the truth of The Man himself that sets all free; so, it is here we should necessarily begin.

Humble, sincere, and boldly fearless in our seeking of our own Selves, individually and collectively, for we are each but parts to the greater whole that is, *us*.

We must focus our efforts upon *Man, our very concept of such a, thing,* applying what we accept we know now in this modern age, *in a new way,* to perceive truth that *has been before us from the beginning, yet hidden by ignorance and animality, made worse by hubris and fear.*

The simple remedy remains: *awareness of these truths of our Self.*

> *The idea that a remedy does not act unless its origin is known is extremely widespread. To quote Erland Nordenskiold again: "Every magical chant must be preceeded by an incantation telling the origin of the remedy used, otherwise it does not act... For the remedy or the healing chant to have its effect, it is necessary to know the origin of the plant, the manner in which the first woman gave birth to it."*
>
> M. Eliade|Myth and Reality

Awareness of origin, cures all ailments; *thus it is truth of The Man that shall cure this world of the ailment that, he yet remains to be.*

...as in the Vainamoinen myth given above, the origin of remedies is closely connected with the history of the origin of the World.

M. Eliade|Myth and Reality

—Resnik

15

OUR ART

And that our art doth further

B. Jonson|The Alchemist

Not all the secret and esoteric organizations of the modern world include entrance rites or initiation ceremonies. Initiation is usually reduced to instruction obtained from a book.

M. Eliade|Rites and Symbols

...bringing it all to life in a way for ordinary people to understand.
DeLonge, Levenda|Sekret Machines, Gods

SEEKER,

Presently, contemplating the thought that, "*To The Stars*", is naught but an attempt to "*initiate the un-initiated*"; [what would appear in-fact to be, *the entirety of The Village*].

Those still seeking the proverbial *Disclosure, unconsciously seek naught but their own Initiation. It is a...thirst; —and the Western World is fucking parched.*

An interesting attempt if so; unfortunately though, it would indeed "come-up-short", in that, *the mythology apparently subscribed to through a belief by DeLonge et al., still seems ...Ancient, ...Primordial; ...Chaotic.*

Their interest is chiefly sociological and psychological; they illustrate the disorientation of a part of the modern world, the desire to find a substitute for religious faith. They also illustrate the indomitable inclination toward the mysteries, the occult, the beyond—an inclination that is an integral part of the human being and that is found in all ages on all levels of culture, especially in periods of crisis.

M. Eliade|Rites and Symbols Of Initiation

Borges points out diabolically that as the belief in Tlon grows, our own society, which doesn't know that there is no such thing as Tlon, will start producing its own spurious hronir, pseudo facts and quasi memories of Tlon that will slowly replace the old reality.

J. Vallee|Revelations

Thus, this attempt to *"Initiate the masses"*, is but *just another of a very, very long line of, similar attempts by sundry organizations of Mankind throughout his own history.*

...the success of these enterprises likewise proves man's profound need for initiation, regeneration, and participation in the life of spirit.
M. Eliade|Rites and Symbols Of Initiation

This attempt to "make aware", *"enlighten" The People of The Tribe*, awakening them to the *"spiritual side of, Things"* [again], is itself a *very archaic practice* indeed, and the Media Outreach and *pressure applied upon the political leaders of the village* by this *self-believed "Magician" and his council of merry men* is but another, modern attempt by Secret Societies and Organizations of Mankind, to wrest control of Life and the Cosmos from the hands of the common man, who has always unwittingly held a firm grasp of that unknown darkness he still fears.

This is, a tired game of cosmic children that the *true wise Man* giggles at from a distance; this, play-pretend, of the children-of-men.

The frightening, even terrifying fact, says Borges, is that the unknown masters of Orbis Tertius are slowly substituting their own reality for ours.

J. Vallee|Revelations

To be sure, we find today a considerable number of secret sects, secret societies, pseudo-initiatory groups, hermetic or neospiritualistic movements, and the like...It is no new phenomenon. Interest in occultism, accompanied by a tendency to form more or less secret societies or groups, already appears in Europe in the sixteenth century and reaches its height in the eighteenth.

M. Eliade|Rites and Symbols Of Initiation

When you're peddling shite on every corner, you no longer desire to truly change the world.

In fact, *neither do you belong to any truly "secret society" as you may fantasize yourself belonging, in your childish play-pretend reality; nay, you* seek only to change *the weight of your own ignorant animal pockets, at the literal expense of the Life-Force of all other.* Indeed, a dark, unconscious, and severely lacking depth-perception, yet ails even the, supposed, most modern thinking and self-professed angelic of us all.

Lost Boy: Come on, Rufio, hit him back.
Rufio: Mung Tongue.
Peter: Math tutor.
Rufio: Pinhead.
Peter: Prison barber.
Rufio: Mother lover.
Peter: Nearsighted Gynecologist

"Hook", 1991

Most of these *Disclosure Artists*, [as they always do], have supposed "good intentions": just like the child who, intends no harm when caring for and loving his family of hamsters by, *unconsciously in that spirit of love, squeezing the literal life out of each; in fact suffocating the damned things*...ignorantly, childishly wielding the strength of a Man, while harboring the unacknowledged disposition of an animal.

> *It is not surprising that critics are increasingly attracted by the religious implications, and especially by the initiatory symbolism, of modern literary works. Literature plays an important part in contemporary civilization.*
> M. Eliade|Rites and Symbols Of Initiation

Good intentions are not enough, if the foundation is built of Cotton-Candy. Standby for a necessary interruption of nutritious voices:

> *If the Earth is likened to a Mother, all the things that she carries in her bowels are homologous with embryos, or living beings in course of "gestation" —that is, of growth and development. This conception is very clearly expressed in the mineralogical terminology of the various traditions. For example, the Indian treatises on mineralogy describe the emerald in its "matrix" in the rock as an embryo.*
> M. Eliade|Myths, Dreams and Mysteries

> *By the fourth century, the constitution of the Arcana Disciplina, the "secret teaching", is complete; in other words, the idea that the Christian mysteries are to be guarded from the uninitiated finally triumphs. As Hugo Rahner expresses it, "The mysteries of baptism and the sacrificial altar were surrounded with a ritual of awe and secrecy, and soon the iconostasis concealed the holy of holies from the eyes of the non-initiate: these became... 'mysteries that make men freeze with awe'."*
> M. Eliade|Rites and Symbols Of Initiation

The foolish dramas of fraternity and military hazings increasingly miss and obscure the actual need to experience "spiritual hazards". Unguided by ritual elders and genuine spiritual aims, all groups become simple "gangs".

The radical dismantling of institutions, boundaries, beliefs and ecosystems that characterizes the end of an era is an extended funeral that we can consciously attend or try to deny. At some level, we each know that huge shifts in nature and culture are affecting us daily. But without some spiritual vision and ritual structure, we lose the capacity to handle death and embrace life fully. Instead, we build walls of denial to hold off terror and confusion and try to cover our helplessness with displays of force and greed. Denial arises as a primary symptom of the age because of the scope of changes already under way and as a defense against the flood of losses and endings.

M. Meade, Mythologist

I've seen your face before my friend
But I don't know if you know who I am
Well, I was there and I saw what you did
I saw it with my own two eyes
So you can wipe off that grin,
I know where you've been
It's all been a pack of lies

Phil Collins|In The Air Tonight

The desire to behave in the manner of a spirit signifies above all the desire to assume a superhuman condition; in short, to enjoy the freedom, the power, and the knowledge of the supernatural beings,

whether gods or spirits. The shaman obtains this transcendent con-
dition by submitting to an initiatory scenario...

M. Eliade|Rites and Symbols Of Initiation

...throughout religious history, sensory activity has been used as a
means of participating in the sacred and attaining to the divine...
Alchemy was pursued within this same spiritual horizon. The al-
chemist takes up and completes the work of Nature, working at the
same time to "perfect" himself. Gold is the noblest metal because it
is perfectly "mature"...

M. Eliade|Myths, Dreams and Mysteries

Stopped into a church, I passed along the way
Well, I got down on my knees, And I pretend to pray
You know the preacher likes the cold, He knows I'm gonna stay

The Mamas and The Papas|California Dreamin'

There is no guidance in your kingdom
Your wicked walk in Babylon
There is no wisdom to your freedom
The richest man in Babylon

Thievery Corporation|The Richest Man In Babylon

So why do I have the feeling that I am not watching a genuine new
spiritual movement here, but a well-orchestrated puppet show?

J. Vallee|Revelations

16

THE TECHNIQUE

A divide, Calling all the faithless in flight
What am I? I am only dust in this light
But I would like to find another way to find you here
Nation of Language|The Wall & I

Those who play these games should become more imaginative, more
creative, more fully able to gain access to their capacities and to use
their capacities proactively. The players should achieve a new image
of man as a creature of enormous and unfolding potentials.

The players should become increasingly hopeful that the powers
of the human being are sufficient to deal with the problems that
confront us. The players should emerge from these games convinced
that man is not something we know has to be surpassed; rather, man
is still something to be realized.
Masters, Houston|Mind Games

The psychological effects on observers and experiencers is so pro-
found, so life-altering, that this seems to be the whole point of the
experience rather than merely a side effect.
DeLonge, Levenda|Sekret Machines, Gods

What an anthropologist calls a "trance," a psychologist might call
"dissociation," or a scholar of religion "participation mystique," or
even "channeling." Altered states have nebulous borders.

E. Davis|High Weirdness

I dreamed a wind that would sweep
Every castle made of sand
Out across the old far holy land

Edward Sharpe|If I Were Free

RESNIK,

So, I have developed a really awesome method to get myself into a trance-state; a meditative, altered-state of consciousness.

I think that if everyone just did what I do, then *boom*, everyone else will be happy and know what I know about life.

I have a whole list of possible outcomes that are almost always some of the time going to be experienced by others also, if they practice this new method of self-hypnosis I have designed.

I've always been a guru at heart, Resnik.

It's my passion, truly, to help others. If only they just lived how I do and thought the way I did, then it would be so easy!

I'm thinking about writing a book myself, with the 72 steps I've developed that will for the first time in history, *save people*.

—[*Insert your name here.*]

***

'Member what we said back in June
If we still here now then we gotta move

Flora Cash|They Own This Town

Seeker,

Humbly; sincerely, I always appreciate reading and hearing of experiences and, organically developed techniques for *encountering, those* experiences.

History is, *literally,* [not just filled *with*, but], *begun by* naught other than Man reaching toward this *Sacred Beyond* which he intuits to be ...there... *somewhere*, and then sharing that intuited data with all others who dare listen.

Man has shared, *and continues to do so at an ever more rapid pace*, his many methods for accessing, *The Beyond; The Abyss.* Indeed, he has been doing so from *The Beginning.*

This reveals a truth.

The truth, that while Man loves to *share, and in fact should and, could not do otherwise,* ...his sharing is for naught else than his own Self, *primarily*; his own effort. Just another of infinite reflections.

There are, many paths; and, we are, *each, It.*

Sharing individual technique has never, and shall never, be *enough* to rattle the cages and bring new life to a stillborn world.

We must actually, *actively discourage*, all others from a direct copy of our own methods for reaching out to *The Beyond,* and greatly *encourage* each other to further develop and grow *their* already inherent and perhaps atrophied or misunderstood methods for, this contact.

Indeed, many times all that is needed is a *surrender* to what is intuited to have already been happening all along, *in The Dark; unconsciously.*

Our individual techniques can be signposts along *The Way,* blindingly aflame for sure. Clean hands with trimmed nails, pointing our own way, that all the other might simply, observe that it is *possible.*

A free and fearless sharing of our own experience and *knowing*, with the humble understanding that, while we wish "*our way*" was "*The Way*" for all those others, the beauty here [*hear!*], is that, *each man and woman already have all they shall ever need, to gain access to this infinite storehouse*, and, *it requires no faith or belief or hope in anything or anyone other than, your own divinely-evolved Self:* your very own cosmically-interconnected, *Being.*

Your essence, is, the same as that of the cosmos itself, thus, we each, are, *that...now aware.*

I share here a remembrance of a lesson, Seeker, learned so very long ago, taught to me by none other than *The Empire* itself, in the course of my own young initiation into the higher-realms of a dying art; that of, *pattern recognition and application.*

A lesson, so vital to the psyche of the initiate, and yet so few actually grasp the freedom it truly allows; the lesson, passed orally and repeatedly:

> *"You mustn't teach technique. Each one of*
> *us must develop his own, Modus Operandi,*
> *that he might ensure the safe and efficient*
> *guidance of his fellow Man, into a shared*
> *and, brightly-lit future."*

Thus, while there is value for all, in the individual technique, [*in that, we may perceive through reflection in each-other, greater truths of our own Selves*], the true wealth of a *Technique*, is for none but that individual himself.

We mustn't teach *Technique*, but simply encourage its development within each and all, which makes it, *tech*nically-un*ique*.

Each and all are *their own doorway; portal to, the sacred; the beyond.* Each must discover and uncover, through struggle primarily, a way to open this doorway. *The Techniques and Schools and Programs are always and primarily for, the creator of such a supposed Technique.*

Our techniques are always our own, primarily, as you should now wisely intuit. Interestingly, history is *full of fools,* who, lick and suck and grope and grind all over the sundry fingers of self-professed gurus, distracted by the fleshy appendages, not seeing that all fingers point to the same one moon.

These fools suck the pointing fingers of others, rather than the moon itself, in which the finger has always pointed. Thank you, Alan Watts.

For each *Technique* points toward, *that warm inviting mammary of the Moon we each so desperately and darkly grope for.*

We each have within us, the drive to seek *that comforting milk of The Beyond* from whence we are both come and destined to return. Yet, we needn't wait: for we may awake, to realize, we each within us, *are* this *Comforting Moon and Blazing Sun.* That, we can unite these two cosmic forces, thus manifesting the portal we each seek and *are*; encouraging the new reality, we already intuit to be encroaching upon us rapidly.

Whatever its meanings, the concept of consciousness grew to outsize proportions in the imagination of the sixties counterculture. ...By the seventies, what Timothy Leary called the "consciousness movement" had mutated into a "consciousness industry." Techniques, technologies, and all manner of discourses were brought to bear on the elusive and yet ever-present stuff.

E. Davis|High Weirdness

Waking up is harder than it seems
Lera Lynn|The Only Thing Worth Fighting For

I have not, Seeker, a *Technique,* because I have already, long ago realized, that, I *am, The Technique. My very Being, my presence here* [*hear*] *is, the fucking technique.*

I *am,* The Portal. I *am,* The Beyond. *I am, Sun and Moon as One; thus, I am.*

Believe in what your heart is saying
Hear the melody that's playing
There's no time to waste
There's so much to celebrate
Believe in what you feel inside
And give your dreams the wings to fly
You have everything you need
If you just believe

Josh Groban|Believe

This, necessarily sounds like nonsense, only to those fearful *manimals* whom cannot, yet, *truly See and Hear.* We must continue, always, to *fear not;* for this is all easily remedied.

Indeed, *the cold chill* [that tends to tingle along the spine at encountering such bold words], *can be warmed!* Ignited; aflame in one's own irradiating and growing core of molten awareness.

Modern man can, and therefore must, live with unprecedented self-awareness. Perhaps the task of living has become more difficult—but there is no way around it.

R. Arnheim|Art and Visual Perception

I walk, breathe, love, fuck, play, create, write, chew, digest, and shit, in a hyper-state of active, contemplative, advanced awareness. *Life for my Self is, lived, in a perpetual state of meditation, without deviation.*

No point in the figure is free from this influence. Granted there are "restful" spots, but their restfulness does not signify the absence of active forces. "Dead Center" is not dead. No pull in any one direction is felt when pulls from all directions balance one another. To the sensitive eye, the balance of such a point is alive with tension. Think of a rope that is motionless while two men of equal strength are pulling it in opposite directions. It is still, but loaded with energy.

R. Arnheim|Art and Visual Perception

I am, The Technique, and, this truth of my own, reveals to my Self that, *this is true for each and all other: that, each and every of us, are the technique for making contact with The Beyond which, we each indeed are, yet heretofore have realized, not.*

There is a dis-connect; and, each must seek to re-connect by, tying an inner knot.

—Resnik

In this sense, ASCs establish themselves relationally, in conjunction with a lively and interactive Beyond, some inside-outside dimension of reality that seems to have something to say…The point is that the anthropological experience of ASCs often takes the form of an encounter, an "I-Thou" relationship that demands a communica-

tive attitude in situ. That's where the high weirdness often begins. The inner empiricist finds that she is not alone.

E. Davis|High Weirdness

Oh I've been contained
But there's a power here to be set free
My love, Won't you just look in my eyes
See what lies behind the mirror of
A modern life don't suit my. My stripes

Marsh|My Stripes

It's coming, the moment, we waited, for so long
We have it, we're on it, we'll have it, I promise

Flora Cash|They Own This Town

Won't you come down
And make me feel happy
It's getting cold, And America's dying
And I know that you know
But I'll keep it a secret

Low Roar|Fucked Up

This is true at any level of education. The art student who copies the manner of an impressive teacher is in danger of losing his intuitive sense of right and wrong in the struggle with a form of representation that he can imitate but not master.

R. Arnheim|Art and Visual Perception

17
EYE SEE, YOU

Illuminating love falls from the skies
To water the illusions in our eyes
All that we desire and all we fear
All our aspirations grow unclear
We feel endlessly, Beyond all gravity
Who are we, What we see
I can't comprehend

Thievery Corporation|All That We Perceive

...I endeavor to show that the tendency toward the simplest struc-
ture, the development by stages of differentiation, the dynamic
character of percepts, and other fundamentals apply to each and
every visual phenomenon....and I hope that a more explicit insis-
tence on their ubiquitous presence will let the reader see the many
aspects of shape, color, space, and movement more compellingly as
manifestations of one coherent medium.

R. Arnheim|Art and Visual Perception

Everything's so blurry

Puddle Of Mudd|Blurry

SEEKER,

...a random thought, just now;...

If studied, would those who've seen UFO, UAP, USO and all other of the sundry light displays and super-natural phenomena, prove to be: *Right-Eye Dominant*, or, *Left-Eye Dominant?*

> *For what seemed an immensely long time I gazed without knowing,*
> *even without wishing to know, what it was that confronted me.*
>   A. Huxley|The Doors Of Perception

—*Resnik*

***

RESNIK,

Eye dominance? *Never heard of it! That just seems...weird.*
—[*Insert your name here.*]

***

> *It was odd, of course, to feel that "I" was not the same as these arms*
> *and legs "out there", as this wholly objective trunk and neck and*
> *even head. It was odd; but one soon got used to it. And anyhow*
> *the body seemed perfectly well able to look after itself. All that the*
> *conscious ego can do is to formulate wishes, which are then carried*
> *out by forces which it controls very little and understands not at all.*
>   A. Huxley|The Doors Of Perception

SEEKER,

All those who've both professionally and exceedingly-adequately discharged the stored energy of their weapon of death from distance, know, the eye with which the Marksman perceives, *does necessarily matter.*

Indeed, as does the efficient dealer of death, the artist likewise knows the eye with which one perceives, either *inspires*, or *confuses*, and is not surprised when become aware of both happening at once.

Not only, Seeker, are we aware of ocular dominance, but it would now indeed seem to be the case that *such asymmetry is a necessary imbalance encouraging growth*:

> *In human vision, the brain has to select one view of the world from our two eyes. However, the existence of a clear anatomical asymmetry providing an initial imbalance for normal neural development is still not understood...Although apparently anatomically symmetrical, our two eyes, which are strongly connected to the brain, exhibit rivalry and dominance...Deprivation has shown competition between the two eyes from birth...The presence or absence of asymmetry in fovea at birth and throughout development seems to play a pivotal role in the neural connectivity of the brain...*
> Le Floch, Ropars|Left-Right Asymmetry

Considering whether and how ocular dominance would impact reports of phenomena such as *The UFO*, we need only consider:

> *...monocular deprivation has shown the importance of competition in the functional development of the complex nervous pathways and synapses, especially during the critical period. Among the different sense inputs to the human brain, each optic nerve consists of 1.2 million fibers, while each auditory nerve a mere 30,000.*
> Le Floch, Ropars|Left-Right Asymmetry

Thus, ocular-dominance is literally a pathway for us to follow to the animal brain, realizing upon arrival that, we are often subject to our own interference;

"cross-talk" making us equally at all times subject to our own deception. We then can, without slightest hesitation, assume those in the world whose goals are to keep secrets and create weapons of a stealthy nature, *would have knowledge of such functioning of the Human System.*

These sorts of weaknesses are necessarily and always exploited for the benefit of men-of-deception. Weak-*spots*, turned into *points*, of entry, in which to manipulate *The Man.*

> *The lack of asymmetry in dyslexics perturbs the complex connectivity and lateralization of the different modal and cross-modal regions of the brain involved in reading and other tasks.*
>
> *The retinal connectivity, the organization and the detailed topography of the primary cortex, along with the columnar architecture can be affected, but also numerous superior bundles such as the corpus callosum, the magnocellular pathway, and the left arcuate fasciculus where converging cross-modal interaction of phonemes and graphemes is observed.*
>
> Le Floch, Ropars|Left-Right Asymmetry

> *We have neglected the gift of comprehending things through our senses. Concept is divorced from percept, and thought moves among abstractions. Our eyes have been reduced to instruments with which to identify and to measure; hence we suffer a paucity of ideas that can be expressed in images and an incapacity to discover meaning in what we see.*
>
> R. Arnheim|Art and Visual Perception

> *...if someone put two plates together, and then there seems to be almost like a small funnel of IR energy that's at the top and the bottom of those plates. There's a stick going in between two plates, but not that pronounced. So, there's an energy field that kind of*

went to a funnel on the top and the bottom, ...at least that was what the FLIR [footage] was showing.

R. Graves|US Navy Pilot

Necessarily because of my own previous training and profession, I have been both exposed to and, required to be familiar with, a vast assortment of what I call *aeroforms*, from all sectors and activity of humanity. From peasant to president, *known* to *yet-unknown*, secret to top-secret, military to civilian, experimental to established.

What I mean to say, is that when I have seen anything supposed-to-be *"Unidentified"*, I am sufficiently equipped to *immediately identify said aeroform, in any number of ways*, thus when any *truly* phenomenal craft-like form appears in *vision* or *dream*, it arrives in any of the well known forms I already have collected within me as a "Thing" of awareness; *the concepts within, that, construct my reality moment to moment;* [a way of saying, naught remains "unidentified" to my Self].

When approached by anything novel manifesting *externally*, it has always, necessarily, made itself known via simple, brilliantly illumined, *"Light In The Sky"* phenomena.

All this to express that, from a young age *I have been immunized against the standard, ubiquitous rotating craft known as The Saucer, or any other supposed "out of this world" appearing, thing.*

Indeed, all thanks to *The Empire,* I have *a diverse catalogue of aeroform concepts* "to pull from", so to say. Thus, when any supposed *Other Worldly* attempts to grab my attention manifest, they are in *familiar and known forms,* or, *the brilliantly divine light.*

With which [I], do [you] seek?

[E]mbrace [Y]our [E]volution. Seeker.

—*Resnik*

...the subject matter of the picture is an integral part of the structural conception. Only because shapes are recognized as head, body, hands, chair, do they play their particular compositional role. The fact that the head harbors the mind is at least as important as its shape, color, or location...Man and animal are sufficiently bilateral creatures to have trouble in telling left from right, b from d.

R. Arnheim|Art and Visual Perception

The world is an illusion of dreams
We're playing roles in silent movies
Why do we hide?
Nothing is real and you'll disappear
Could we let go of all our fears?

Thievery Corporation|No More Disguise

END CALL

Seeker,

Surely at this point in our *conversation* together, we can agree now that perhaps we have, *all*, been taking this subject a bit too seriously. Complicating this life unnecessarily.

Until next time, Seeker; may you grasp the message, embrace your own evolution, and become what you have always been: *free*.

—*Resnik*

When you get the message, hang up the phone...The biologist does not sit with eye permanently glued to the microscope; he goes away and works on what he has seen.

A. Watts|The Joyous Cosmology

VOICE MEMOS

PHILOSOPHOETIC:
*[Deception]
*[UAP]
*[Missed Machinations]
*[Besos de Noche]
*[The Signs]

   RESNIK'S ABYSS:
*[Entry]

DECEPTION

Give me the superstitions of a nation, and I care not who makes their laws, or who writes their music.

M. Twain

SEEKER; I ACKNOWLEDGE THIS truth; *the Perception* of his fellow Man; his Self; that, I accept Mr. Twain understood what, he was stating; that how easily we are, in our animalness, *deceived*; that, Man is surely one of the most, uniquely, intelligent creatures of *the Universe*, yet we, remain so beautifully childlike, in our ignorance of, ourself.

Whoever wants to see will see badly. It was my will that deceived me. It was my will that provoked the huge uproar among the daimons.

C. G. Jung|Liber Novus

Realize; that, there are significant patterns, you, unknowingly follow; an automaton; that, you may yet intelligently maneuver, within these patterns; *the Programming.*

I'm saying that there's always someone behind things that don't seem to have an explanation.

C. Liu|The Three-Body Problem

Is there a science of deception at work here on a grand scale...
                              J. Vallee|Passport To Magonia

Understand; Mr. Twain perceived, what many elite politicians, are now, today, aware of; that, many a CEO know; Advertiser; and, *War Pig*; that, when you acknowledge *the Patterns*, you, are thus enabled access; that, there are schematics for your control.

...that I must discover, at all costs, some manner or means for destroying in people the predilection for suggestibility which causes them to fall easily under the influence of "mass hypnosis".
                              G. I. Gurdjieff

Seeker; you are very easily deceived; frighteningly so; that, you will not admit it; that, part of *the Deception*, is, your *arrogance*, in avoiding any sincere, contemplation as to the, possibility, of its, applicability, to yourself; that, you will internally agree to the, suggestion, of, the susceptibility to *deception*, in which your *brother; neighbor; spouse; children; political-opponents*; and *coworkers*, routinely fall prey.

Pride, where wit fails, steps in to our defense, And fills up all the mighty void of sense.
                              A. Pope|Essay On Man

Realize; that, you hubristically deny such a scenario, for *yourself*; that, you believe yourself far too intelligent, and, capable of a creature; that, you have accumulated absurd amounts, of debt, in pursuit of a *higher*-education, that, shields you, magically, from this *deception*; manipulation.

Understand; regardless of your acknowledgment, and acceptance of, *the Truth*, Mr. Twain reveals to us, changes not *the Story*; that, there are those among you, who, use this as an advantage; that, many indeed prefer, that, you not accept, what is being posited here.

Opinions too soon formed often deflect
man's thinking from the truth into gross error,
in which his pride then binds his intellect.

It is worse than vain for men to leave the shore
and fish for truth unless they know the art;
for they return worse off than they were before.

D. Alighieri|The Divine Comedy

Seeker; much has happened in the recent history of Mankind; that, within the last 100 years alone, Man has, exponentially increased in number; that, it is indeed difficult to track and sort so many, billions of creatures; that, there are pockets of people; fellow men; who are aware of our collective vulnerability, to *deception*; that, these decide continually; in all epochs; to exploit this vulnerability.

Seeker; *fear*, is indeed a very powerful motivating force; that, regardless of office held or economic status; Man is full of fear; that, this fear motivates powerful men to do, terrible things; secret things; manipulative things; *deceptive* things, to his fellow Man; that, your arrogance prevents you from, *seeing*, these patterns of *deception*.

Bread of deceit is sweet to a man; but afterwards his mouth shall
be filled with gravel.

Proverbs 20:17|KJV

Seeker; we are again, today, in this most modern epoch of Man, discussing amongst ourselves; *the Return of the Gods*; that, there are increasing rumors once again, spreading, amongst certain pockets of, Mankind, of *non*-human intelligence, in control of flying machines. That, Man has a belief that he is not alone; that, this belief can be fear disguised; that, Man longs for comfort; security; that, *we always have; especially today*; that, *the Child* that is Mankind, seeks the, comfort of a mother and father; a higher-authority; that, you believe this life to be, far too scary and mysterious, to face alone; that, you think Man is surely too irresponsible, to be given charge of such a grand garden; that, Man has but one recourse for, psychological stability; that, we create and suppose a, further, advanced, anthropomorphic entity, charged, with responsibility for, Mankind; that, again you agree that, most around, you, require and, would benefit, in receiving assistance from, a higher-authority; yet, not accept that, you likewise, esoterically desire the same. That, just as we are birthed into *the Lap* of, our mother, we likewise as adults seek, the cosmic lap of comfort; a higher-authority that will shelter and, protect us, and, one day, show to us that, all is in order; *all is well*; that, Man is watched over; that, Man is special.

> *Bird: We'll fetch help from the clouds trailing above your head, when nothing else is of help to us.*
> *I: You want to fetch help from the clouds? How is that possible?*
>
> C. G. Jung|Liber Novus

Realize; ouroboros. That, this has all happened many times; that, are we now evolved enough to realize our truth?

He who fails to acknowledge, empowers those who, seek to control him. That, as you desire control of, your spouse; your children; your pet; your body and mind; your peers and coworkers; as you secretly desire to control, every aspect of your life, *in ever expansive and increasing ways*, there are men, far in advance of you; that, some members of our grand species have, been intelligently engineering ways to employ, *deception*, as a means of control; advantage; as you likewise both desire and practice in, your own small daily ways.

Seeker; what is really going on? What is the Motive behind recent revelations in, the Western world? That, military aviators perceive flying candy, in, the Skies; breath-mints? That, political leaders open their doors to, men, of deception.

> *No country has won a war in the face of enemy air superiority, no major offensive has succeeded against an opponent who controlled the air, and no defense has sustained itself against an enemy who had air superiority.*
>
> Col. J. A. Warden III|U.S. Air Force

Realize; when you look backward, behind us, along the dark trail of chaos and creativity that is, Man; what is the trend?; what are *the Patterns?*

Understand; we are nothing if not creatures of habit; that, indeed we are creatures, as susceptible to, *self*-training in our habitual, patterned ways, as any of our brethren of the animal kingdom.

Seeker; has anything substantially changed in the habits, and patterns of, Man? That, we have merely adorned ourselves in, modern garb and meme; unwittingly still in an ouroboros of psychoses; wandering down distantly archaic, yet, frighteningly close and familiar, archetypal, labyrinths of psyche, in our, unconscious, behavior and patterns of thought.

> *When faced with a totally new situation, we tend always to attach*
> *ourselves to the objects, to the flavor of the most recent past. We look*
> *at the present through a rear-view mirror. We march backward*
> *into the future.*
>
> M. McLuhan|The Medium Is The Massage

Seeker; what does a people; a tribe; a nation, do, *after*, multiple generations of war? Specifically, what does a nation do after, *World War?* What does an only modern super-power do, after a *Cold War*, and, subsequent collapse, of a *Soviet Union?* What do weapons manufacturers do, with but just, a handful of nations, capable of, sustaining their business of death? That, *the United States of the West* are, left, the sole apparent super-power; that, how does *the Military* stay proficient, *without an enemy?* That, how does *the Tradecraft* of espionage, continue to sharpen, *without a stone in which, to grind?*

> *We're talkin' danger*
> *We're talkin' danger, baby*
> *Like stranger in Moscow*
>
> *I'm living lonely*
> *I'm living lonely, baby*
> *Stranger in Moscow*
>
> M. Jackson|HIStory

Seeker; it is imperative that you, *think differently; about everything;* do not be afraid; you are capable; that, does the Super-Power, *being super*, turn to, *itself? Would you?*

Realize; it would be decided amongst a few; that, the suggestion would be, for the independent, branches of defense and intelligence, to agree; in effort to stay ready, *nay*, to improve and, grow stronger, there must be an understanding that, to be ready, for all possibilities, *the United-States* must turn, on itself. That, unknown to all but a small group, *the U.S.* military after the Cold War, was forced to wage battle upon, itself; that, a *concept* developed through witnessing, the Athletics Department; that, Navy vs. Air Force, or, Army vs. Marine, *was no longer just sport; it was expanded into the real world of, combat preparation and proving; an initiatory ordeal ala Mircea Eliade; a bit of friendly competition, at first perhaps; however, easily and quickly evolved out-of-hand; rapidly;* that, there would be a moment; a point reached; a singularity; allowing for the game to grow to a size, unfriendly to that of containment; that, the Game became so beneficial to, growth, it organically evolved into a, complex organism, now indistinguishable, from any *actual* outside threat; that, in your desire to *stay sharp* during peacetime, you have unwittingly *cut yourself.*

> *He also knew there existed a long-standing rivalry between scientists at SRI and at Livermore and remembers wondering, "Was this some kind of confidence trick?"*
>
> A. Jacobsen|Phenomena

Seeker; as this monster; *Golem;* evolved, private corporations, contracted and, paid by *the Military*, to assist in the efforts to, keep *the Tip* of the *Spear* sharp, likewise, quickly reached, an understanding; an equilibrium, with, competing technology and, weapons manufacturers; that, all may be fair in the game of war; and, business; that, in order to satisfy the requirements, of, *the Government*; an *internal* sort of cold-war developed; a *game*; a *competition*; an, *evolution*.

How far would private corporations go, to, *succeed?; advance?; gain?;* that, *this is the sole purpose of such an entity!;* that, *how far do, you, go?*

Seeker; what are *the Patterns* of human behavior with, technological advances? Is there a reliable pattern of, technological proliferation for the sole *benefit* of Mankind? Is there a pattern of, *greed; deception; war*? That, is there a *secret* war being waged? *Cold, Warm, or Hot?* That, would *the Proliferation* of, advanced, technological discoveries, incite military and espionage tactics, between competing corporations charged with developing weapons for, *the Super-Power?* That, would our outdated politicians have any clue? Would the greater, youthful body of, *the D.O.D.*, and, *the Intelligence* agencies, have any sort of grasp, on a *secret technology war?*

> *Real, total war has become information war. It is being fought by subtle informational media—under cold conditions, and constantly. The Cold War is the real war front—a surround—involving everybody—all the time—everywhere. Whenever hot wars are necessary these days, we conduct them in backyards of the world with the old technologies. These wars are happenings, tragic games. It is no longer convenient, or suitable, to use the latest technologies for fighting our wars, because the latest technologies have rendered war meaningless. The hydrogen bomb is history's exclamation point. It ends an age-long sentence of manifest violence.*
>
> M. McLuhan|The Medium Is The Massage

Realize; certainly they would have hunches; that, they'd have strange debris fall from, *the Sky*, which, always manages to be, just a few, decades ahead of the *supposed reality* of, the standard-issue military of old. That, just as surely as the world's largest, *consumer-level* technology corporations, sit, upon several generations of advanced technology; tucked away in *the Laboratory*; that, the weapons corporations charged, with developing weapons platforms for, *the Empire*; the greatest super-powered civilization, and military, this planet has yet known, *are likewise sitting upon a stockpile*, of advanced technological plans, and concepts; that, while *the Pilots* aviate themselves in, *1980's* technology; with, upgraded-electronics-components from, the *90's;* the Laboratory technology is similarly organized as such that, it shan't see *the Light* of day for, many more human generations.

And such devices do exist, either in test sites across the U.S. or on the
drawing boards of various Silicon Valley firms and Washington
think tanks.

J. Vallee|Revelations

Understand; the oblivious political and military authorities, would, also have endless reports and embarrassments, surrounding what *the Public* and *the Media*, claim to be, unidentified aerial phenomena.

Politics offers yesterday's answers to today's questions.
M. McLuhan|The Medium Is The Massage

Seeker; when would they realize, they were chasing, their own tails [*tales*]; *shadows; ouroboros like?* Would they? *Would, you?*

Understand; injecting more and more of *the Funding*, into secret, private, projects, in hopes to, catch-up with the oft reported, UAP. That, it is their own cash that, both created, and, now sustains the modern beast they chase with their, cameras and sensors; that, *the Chase* you give with your military, weapons and programs, does nothing but, sharpen *the Iron*, of *the Foe* they, unwittingly fund; that, *Artificial-Intelligence* was created, so to speak; *entities*, quickly realizing their own, *superiority to the Father.*

Seeker; what sort of *OSI* type program of infiltration, and, *deception*, would an elite, advanced, technology and weapons corporation, have at its disposal? That, there are multiple corporations, all working, and competing, to keep their secrets hidden from, each-other; that, naturally and necessarily this would indicate, keeping it secret from *the Public*; primarily, *you.*

Seeker; be encouraged to realize; that, *allowing* there to remain, *anything*, *Unidentified* in the skies, in this modern age, only in/ensures a ready-made, pre-baked excuse, to prevent *your* becoming *aware*, of, *brilliantly designed, advanced, human-made contraptions.* That, with a ready-made excuse like, alien visitors, anyone can fly around in any *thing*, without registration, without compulsion to comply with *any boundary restrictions*; that, the primary reaction now of *the Public; as well as military;* is, the ubiquitous UAP; that, to suggest, we as a species, are incapable of, wonderfully magical contraptions, of the likes suggested by *The Phenomenon, simply reveals your atrophied mind.*

> *Power over matter—external reality, as you would call it—is not important. Already our control over matter is absolute... We control matter because we control the mind. Reality is inside the skull. You will learn by degrees, Winston. There is nothing that we could not do. Invisibility, levitation—anything. I could float off this floor like a soap bubble if I wished to. I do not wish to, because the Party does not wish it. You must get rid of those nineteenth-century ideas about the laws of nature. We make the laws of nature.*
>
> G. Orwell|1984

Seeker; *The Philosophoet* knows, the simplest; cheapest; *most effective,* cloaking-technology, is, that which, *avoids the Consciousness,* of, the perceiving mind, *the Observer,* by, *simply,* —*refusing to be named.*

> *In any case, mere control of the features was not enough. For the first time he perceived that if you want to keep a secret you must also hide it from yourself. You must know all the while that it is there, but until it is needed you must never let it emerge into your consciousness in any shape that could be given a name.*
>
> G. Orwell|1984

Seeker; we have allowed *the Fear* to pull us, too far off *the Path;* that, there are intelligent *human* forces, that, take advantage of this; in an effort to, cloak their comings and goings; their, testing and experimenting; *battles.*

Realize; Jacques Vallee vehemently warned *the Public,* of such possibilities; Mr. Vallee himself stated, he was *the Target* of, similar, or the same, groups, while at *the Apex* of his, research and studies of, *the UAP* phenomenon.

Seeker; would Mr. Vallee be able to, indefinitely avoid, *contamination and influence,* by such a motivated and, well funded effort of *deception;* increasing its capabilities and reach, with each, passing decade? *Would you?*

Seeker; what are the trends? *Patterns?* What does known history tell us of ourself? When you grasp the importance of, the patterns, which Mr. Vallee brilliantly alludes to, you, *must instantly begin to think differently*; that, you must step aside, from your pride; your attachment, to career and wealth; and societal standing; that, you must free *yourself* from the, control-scheme, Vallee warned of; that, *old ways of thought, will no longer suffice.*

Seeker; fear not the fate of, the ubiquitous Alien and his craft; that, I have yet begun to speak on the nature and, reality of *the Alien* itself; that, *the essential and pertinent fact here,* is that, whether or not we are being visited, by non-human intelligence, is a question, ultimately unanswerable, until, we remedy the, very *Human* problems of, *deception; manipulation; fear; greed;* to, *name,* but a few of our plagues.

Realize; that, to those charged with authority over the, masses, there are arguably zero true incentives, for identifying an aerial phenomenon; that, contrarily, there remain *sundry* reasons, why these same authorities, would actually, work to ensure such phenomena *remain* unidentified. That, surely there must be a reason why, in this modern era of *the Man,* we have presumed objects of, supposed profane nature, over populated areas, *yet to be catalogued and documented, labeled and researched*; that, the term *Unidentified,* has outworn its use; its value; that, *Unidentified is lazy*; that, *it is a tired excuse*; that, *we should, all, be embarrassed for, entertaining this false concept for so long*; that, Man is what he is, because of his ability, to label; that, it is time to open our eyes, all of us, and, approach life like *the Gods* we surely are; that, if something yet remains to be identified, *realize,* that one of you has, *made it this way for a reason.*

> *The first herring that is caught is showered with compliments and blessings; pompous titles are lavished upon it, and it is handled with the greatest respect and reverence; it is the herring-god!*
>
> J. Weir|Religion and Lust

Realize; there are no longer any acceptable excuses, for *Unidentified*; that, the very term *Unidentified,* should spur within each Man, an impulse, to join *the Game of, cosmic identification.*

..the Lord God formed every beast of the field, and every fowl of
the air; and brought them unto Adam to see what he would call
them: and whatsoever Adam called every living creature, that was
the name thereof.

Genesis 2:19|KJV

Understand; wealth, long-term goals, patience; *what so few of us actually ever possess all at once.* That, you do not butcher the *milk*-producing cow, for *meat*, until it dries up; regardless of how, beefy, it may presently appear to be.

Realize; at a certain point of, accumulation of wealth and, influence, the concerns of the average man, *no longer apply, nor can be appreciated by*, such self-professed elite humans. That, they truly inhabit, a separate sort of reality; that, reaching this point, their outlook extends, many hundreds of generations into *the Future*; that, while most men worry for tomorrow, there are those contemplating, *and already well prepared for*, the next *several hundred years*. That, they *organize, plan*, and *war* for, *the Future*; that, they intend and implement, an increasingly *deceptive, modus operandi*, to insure the extreme, long-term survival, of, *their own* lineage.

Realize; when you have endless finance now; that, when you know your family-line is secure, and supported for, the next *25 generations*, you hide away *the Future* technology, *for the Future*; you set it aside, for the *great, great, grand-children, of your great, great, grandchildren.* That, the common folk argue over scraps, generation after generation, because they lack, that, there are those *without* lack, arguing over, *control*: of not merely *the planet itself*, but *the very rights to evolutionary, dominance, of our grand species, is in play.* That, while an *individual* may, not yet possess the, ability to embrace animal-immortality, the next best thing is, the long-term survival of, the *bloodline*; ensured by, *money; control; deception; manipulation; influence*; that, perhaps *John Galt* grew tired of waiting; that, a super-power is only, super, *until it is not*; that, perhaps there has been a spontaneous, and rapid growth; evolution; *leapfrog*.

From the point of view of our present rulers, therefore, the only
genuine dangers are the splitting-off of a new group of able, under-

employed, power-hungry people, and the growth of liberalism and
skepticism in their own ranks.

G. Orwell|1984

Seeker; the world has changed; that, it continues at an ever increasing, exponential rate; that, our minds must remain as fluid and, flexible, as *the UAP* haunting *the Sky;* that, as *the UAP* phenomenon continues its, majestic, hypnotizing dance, you remain stuck in the muddy soil of, your mind; trapped within, *the Garden,* once tilled at the, hands of your parents and grandparents; beating tired drums; shaking the same rattle; sounding the same sirens; endlessly repeating the tropes of your father, and, those that came before him.

Understand; the true Human; in his nature as much as his label, knows quite well that, while there yet remain, members of our grand species in bonds, both psychological and physical, economic and spiritual, familial and traditional, religious and social; that, while Man maintains his childish arrogance; his domineering ways; that, while Man continues to shed *the Blood,* of his brother and sister; while we continue to senselessly murder, every aspect of the natural world around us; *it matters not* if we are being visited; *it matters not* who lurks; *it matters not* what technology is promised; what dimension or planet is involved; how many wormholes can be, passed-through, before the biological requirements of our own wormhole of bodily-waste-relief becomes urgent; what shape or color other beings might be; what they promise; what we choose to believe; who knows, and who does not. That, *The Philosophoet* knows, *it is all for naught if, Mankind continues along, his same paths, his same patterns, of thought and behavior.*

Of all the causes which conspire to blind
Man's erring judgment, and misguide the mind,
What the weak head with strongest bias rules,
Is PRIDE, the never-failing vice of fools.

A. Pope|Essay On Man

Seeker; it is now beyond time, to begin, thinking differently. That, Bob Dylan warned the waters of change, were rapidly rising; that, those unable to embrace change, would, indeed *sink like a stone*; that, if you think *the Disclosure* and a revelation, of intelligent Aliens or Inter-dimensional beings, solves any of our very *Human problems*, you remain stuck in *ancient* ways of thinking; that, you continue looking up; professing belief and hope in gods, from *the Sky*; gods from elsewhere; *anywhere else*. That, you desire their arrival in the hope they, save the day for Humanity; that, you resist facing the reality that, if we cannot, care for *each-other*, if we cannot accept this thing called *life*; if we cannot realize a united species: we shall not only be unable to, accurately, grasp any sort of, legitimately attempted, contact, any such action would be, ultimately destructive and harmful, for the *vast majority* of Mankind. That, what are *the Patterns?*

Realize; there is not a single other race in the cosmos that, will care more for, the plight of *the Man*, than, Man himself. That, it is but false hope, to await a savior from, *the Beyond*; a race of beings, benevolent, and sent to guide, Mankind, into *the Heavenly* realm of, *advanced technology and abundant wealth*; that, you mark eighteen revolutions around *the Sol*, and do not realize that, as you age further, you have but continued your imaginative, role-playing ways, well into supposed adulthood; trapped, in an illusion of your own doing; allowing.

> *Like a stray child you stand pitifully among the mighty, who hold the threads of your life. You cry for help and attach yourself to the first person that comes your way. Perhaps he can advise you, perhaps he knows the thought that you do not have, and which all things have sucked out of you.*
>
> C. G. Jung|Liber Novus

Seeker; many today *exuberantly* profess their pride, in attaining, what they consider to be, a state of *awake-ness*; only to, *roll-over and fall back asleep*. That, you label yourself as being awake, as opposed to being asleep; that, you fail to be aware of your, *sleepy unawareness; sleep-walking*; that, *clean your Self, Man; you've been drooling!* That, this is all well; however, allow for me to suggest that, rather than waking-up, we all start by, *growing-up*; that, *an awoken child, is yet a child, while a Man who acknowledges, and forfeits, his immature ways, can awaken to more than, mere fantasies and play-pretends.*

Understand; Man must get out of his own way; that, Man must perceive, beyond the realm of, *deception*, originated by his peers; that, first and foremost, Man must, confront, *himself*, if he ever hopes to, truly commune, with his gods; *the Aliens* in *the Shadow*. That, if there *is* other intelligent life, around this wonderful planet of ours, and, that it were in their interest to do so, surely, they would desire equitable and, productive communication, with, the intellectual and morally balanced members, of any species; not the, *bickering, barking, vengeful, spiteful, hateful, ignorant, fearful, arrogant children*; regardless of these children being 6', erect, mammals capable of, speech. That, if you think having an authoritative, government, a barbaric and brutal military, a job, college education, debt, children of your own, and a cereal-box-knowledge of pop-physics, makes you a mature member of *the Species,* do not anticipate personal contact with, any *legitimate* Other.

Seeker; this is a formal invitation and encouragement, *to free your mind, by thinking differently; independently; contrarily.* That, the old dogs of disclosure continue chasing the, *always-just-out-of-reach, unidentified-vehicle,* as it passes by ever so, *teasingly, wantonly;* that, old dogs hubristically fear new tricks, while the young pup, fearlessly desires to learn, *for his own benefit.*

> *All ye beasts of the field, come to devour, yea, all ye beasts in the forest. His watchmen are blind: they are all ignorant, they are all dumb dogs, they cannot bark; sleeping, lying down, loving to slumber. Yea they are greedy dogs which can never have enough, and they are shepherds that cannot understand: they all look to their own way, every one for his gain, from his quarter. Come ye, say they, I will fetch wine, and we will fill ourselves with strong drink; and tomorrow shall be as this day, and much more abundant.*
>
> Isaiah 56:9-12|KJV

Seeker; it is time; *think differently.*
Fear is a powerful motivator; Hubris is a hell of an obstacle.

Thus far, I have characterized a trap as a closed system of attitudes, beliefs, and habits of thought for which one can give an objective demonstration that certain of the beliefs are incorrect and that certain of the attitudes and habits of thought prevent this from being recognized.

P. Watzlawick|The Invented Reality

...the end of an age of deception and terror which has plagued mankind for far too long.

M. Mott|Caverns, Cauldrons, and Concealed Creatures

...she startled him by saying casually that in her opinion the war was not happening. The rocket bombs which fell daily on London were probably fired by the Government of Oceania itself, 'just to keep people frightened.' This was an idea that had literally never occurred to him.

G. Orwell|1984

Men in their fear fly for refuge to mountains or forests, groves, sacred trees or shrines. But those are not a safe refuge, they are not the refuge that frees a man from sorrow.

The Dhammapada

...our national wealth is in the hands of a few North American corporations for whose benefit alone the present military government is maintained.

P. Albizu-Campos

If the Air Force, or any other government organization, has in fact encouraged its agents to act in such ways, then the result is a scandal on the scale of the disinformation and mind-control operations of the Sixties and the Seventies that culminated in the FBI's Cointel-pro and the CIA's MK-Ultra, a very dark chapter in American history.

J. Vallee|Revelations

A dark chapter indeed.

UAP

One morning while her mother was distracted preparing breakfast, she opened the window and noticed a bright object sparkling by the waters edge. Filled with curiosity, she crept outside and saw a diamond the size of a small coconut, dancing with the waves. As her fingers scarcely touched the waters, a huge bubble enveloped her and transported her to the litao's palace in the bottom of the sea.

The Penguin Book of Mermaids

...half-seen in this one flash of light, it has a cosmic extension, and as such is surrounded by an aura of indefinite spatial and temporal extensions.

P. Teilhard de Chardin|The Phenomenon of Man

SEEKER; *THE UAP;* THE marvelous lights, dancing in *the Sky*; your sky; that, they yet haunt you; your awareness, these UAP; these, coordinated-flashes from whence you both arrive and are destined; indeed, where we are each being led. That, you are haunted by your true origin; a haunting that begs your acknowledgement; it begs for you to follow; it guides; helps; gives; commands; civilizes; organizes; teaches; *and then sets free.* It presents a message; nay, it *is the Message*; that, *the UAP* begs of you:

Do not merely seek the Stars, become them;
then, seek your origin; for surely, we shall

unite there, at the Source, together once
again;

That, *the UAP* aims to draw us to *the Center,* of all; *the Light;* circle;
growth; evolution.

UFOs?!

J. Ito|Sensor

The circles are purple, spinning like fireworks, glowing with the
otherworldly dark light that I'm already getting used to here.
Here? Where is here? Why is it a place where I see colors that do
not exist in everyday life?

G. Hancock|Supernatural

Seeker; Man shall eternally seek *the Center;* that, *the Beginning* is our
end; that, *the Beginning* is *the End* of everything; that, *the End* of all is *the*
Beginning; that, all unknowingly seek, a return to origin; all are compelled,
to return to Wholeness; return to *the Beginning;* return to *the Center;* —*the*
End; hear and see!

We shall not cease from exploration. And the end of all our
exploring will be to arrive where we started. And know the place
for the first time.

R. Tarnas|Cosmos and Psyche

Understand; that, this applies to *the Species* at large, as well as you,
an individual, *self*-consciously aware, cosmic *being;* that, *all* life seeks, *the*
Radiant light; both water-born and earth-born; plant and animal alike; *the*
Planet itself, seeks divine warmth.

How radiant in its essence that must be
which in the Sun (where I now was) shows forth
not by it's color but its radiancy.

Though genius, art, and usage stored my mind,
I still could not make visible what I saw;
but yet may you believe and seek to find!

And if our powers fall short of such a height,
why should that be surprising, since the Sun
is as much as any eye has known of light?

D. Alighieri|The Divine Comedy

Seeker; you are, *self* aware, *are you not?* That, perhaps unbeknownst to you, you do indeed have an analog, space-of-mind, in-which, you may set an idea of, yourself, apart; that, within this self-created analog space of, your mind, you are enabled to perceive, *the Imperceptible*; see, what cannot be seen. That, *the End* of life, is *the Beginning* of life; the End of humanity is indeed, our new beginning; that, you shall forever be drawn by, *that true freedom*; further outside of yourself, until you *become* your Self; *cosmos.*

...we have experienced it too often to admit of any further doubt: an
irregularity in nature is only the sharp exacerbation, to the point
of perceptible disclosure, of a property of things diffused throughout
the universe, in a state which eludes our recognition of its presence.
Properly observed, even if only in one spot, a phenomenon necessar-
ily has omnipresent value and roots by reason of the fundamental
unity of the world.

P. Teilhard de Chardin|The Phenomenon of Man

Seeker; Man shall seek further and deeper into *the Universe*; stretching into infinity until we, fade and merge, beautifully and unflinchingly, back into the Folds, of, who and what and where and why and how we truly are; divinely blessed in every way by *the Power*, of our, *true and actual nature*; that, you are but a singular, and as of yet unknowingly, united aspect of *the Universe,* realized and conscious of, *itself.*

Seeker; evolution and your very magical rhythm. That, you are invited to, glimpse for but a moment; that, if you were to sincerely trace your lineage, far, back into *the Dark* abyss we call time, *to the very beginning which we are, eternally, compelled to seek and, inevitably reach;* that, *all; you; us,* and *everything,* both religious and scientific; both spirit and profane; both traditional and homeopathic; both body and mind; mental and physical; black and white; good and bad; sick and healthy; fat and skinny; east and west; north and south; that, each and every concept, word, sign, and symbol, in all and every language of Man, now and yet to be, *both begins and ends at the Source; the Center; the Light.* That, *the Freedom* we were gifted was, indeed, our own doing; yet, unknown at that moment; that, you, working from *the Future,* upon your past; setting in motion that universal impulse; that biological beacon; rhythmically beating in us each; pushing us in any way it can, to continue evolving; continue creating, continue worshipping *the Gods* you surely are; *the Gods* we have lifted up; *the Gods* we have all created, and yet will. That, regardless of name or type, *the UAP* begs you, *follow; higher, further, faster;* that, you must continue to seek *the Beyond;* seek further into, yourself; further into, *the Cosmos;* for both shall surely lead to *that* light, in-which, you seek.

> *...and in the black night she could see nothing but what she thought was a shooting star.*
>
> J. M. Barrie|Peter Pan

Understand; externally or internally, matter it not; that, there are many paths to *the Source;* many a grand Philosopher and Poet, have braved to tear *the Veil,* which reveals these hidden truths; that, your destiny is surely in *the Stars;* a beautiful, majestic, cosmically magical adventure, surely awaits Mankind. That, an adventure, filled with terror and savagery, need not lie ahead for Man, for we may yet alter the present course of, this ancient Ark; that, you are perfect as you are; all is well; that, regardless of your will, each and all are, properly, placed and in motion; worry not.

Seeker; what can we not achieve, when united as a, common species; *one* organism; that, we are as billions of individual, self-conscious brain-cells, each able to both contribute to, and realize, a more grand reality; bigger story; simply by, being aware of it. That, why continue to fight each-other; *why destroy, when we can so easily create?* That, for those matured enough for *the Journey*, we now find ourselves, in an era of Mankind, in which we begin to embark, wholesale, on a new Ark; our very own, naturally grown, *portal to the heretofore unknown*; embracing a new and, whole reality that, shall surely bend to our will, if we but ask nicely; possessing that grace in which, only true gods can manage.

Seeker; while the current and overwhelming cargo-cult, mentality, of *the Western* world today, prays for heaven, in that UAP Disclosure involves the, *superior authority of an alien pilot sent to save humanity with omniscience, technology, and wealth from above for the whole tribe;* that, to the modern UAP disclosure-disciple, the *ultimate* truth, is, a hellish revelation that, UAP disclosure is not a conspiracy involving visitors from elsewhere, here to save or harm us, but that disclosure of *the Alien* and his UAP, is in actuality a revelation of, Mankind and his, continued evolution. That, the true secret has nothing to do with, actual alien visitors; that, the true secret awaiting disclosure is the, knowledge that Man, is not what he believes himself to be; *he is much more.* This, is dangerous to those fearful leaders still seeking control of their peers. That, the fear of Man realizing his full potential, is a far greater threat to the current paradigm, than any alien being could hope to present; that, whether mechanically or ethereally engineered, UAP disclosure is but, the realization that, it was, *Man all along; it always has been.* That, regardless of the depth of your current understanding, or *lack thereof,* Mankind has, always been the common denominator, in all hauntings and happenings; *necessarily so;* that, do not be fooled; do not be deceived; that, Man has always manifested externally, what is, primarily an internal impulse.

> *Then his soul is a lamp whose light is steady, for it burns in a shelter where no winds come.*
>
> Bhagavad Gita

Realize; that, Mankind today is more than capable of creating, indeed breathing life into, what he originally only intuited; that, *the Dreams,* visions, and ideas of our ancestors, were but fleeting flashing thoughts, notes in journals; —*until they weren't.*

The method of communication has nothing more to do with the reality communicated than have the paper and ink of this essay to do with the ideas which they serve to convey. In each case a vehicle of symbols is necessary in order that one mind should communicate with another; But in both cases this is a vehicle of symbols and nothing more.

Everywhere, therefore, the reality may be psychical, and the physical symbolic; everywhere matter in motion may be the outward and visible sign of an inward and spiritual grace.
G. J. Romanes|Mind and Motion and Monism

But mind and reason have the power, by their nature and at their will, to move through every obstacle.
M. Aurelius|Meditations

Exactly what are these objects and where did they fly here from?!
J. Ito|Hanging Blimp

Moreover, I shall give thee a golden plate decorated with a golden snake, whose raised head is holding in its mouth a priceless gem, from which is shed a light of such brilliance, that by it alone you can see at the darkest hour of midnight as well as you can at noon.
W. Petrovitch|Hero Tales and Legends of the Serbians

The deceased are said to be surrounded with a flame-like envelope, but 'some were like the purest full-moon light,...'
M. Booth|The Secret History of The World

Nature can produce mobile, coherent if transient glowing forms that can leave energetic effects.

P. Devereux|Earth Lights

The rider who had heard the voices said, "Yesterday they all spoke, but now they have changed their forms." Suddenly they saw Rainbow who came in the form of a wheel. He asked, "What are you looking for?" "We are searching for our lost people," said the people. Rainbow warned them, "Don't look at me or you'll become one-eyed."

A. Metraux

Missed Machinations

I didn't see it
I can't believe it
Oh, but I feel it
When you sing to me

M. Anthony|You Sang To Me

We have to prepare ourselves to view the actual mechanisms of ESP
quite independent of the old labels...

I. Swann

Many ESP impressions come as sensory-like impressions...

C. Tart

My senses exist only to feel her.

J. Ito|Sensor

Seeker; *are you, listening?*

   Embrace your own silence; that you might for the first time, truly, —hear ...and
see.

In the Germanic or Japanese men's secret societies, the strange sounds, like the masks, attest the presence of the ancestors, the return of the souls of the dead.
M. Eliade|Rites and Symbols of Initiation

Embrace your evolution, for, *Life*, speaks clearly, —*to those that, Listen.*

Humming in my ears and a small feeling like a warning.
J. Jaynes|The Origin of Consciousness

A tremendous sense of inner tension developed in the subjects—to a degree that volunteers did not believe their bodies were capable of containing it. This buildup of inner tension was accompanied most often by similarly building high-pitched whining, ringing, or crackling sounds.
R. Strassman|Inner Paths to Outer Space

If I activate my sensors, I might find out what it is.
J. Ito|Sensor

There is nothing that can prepare you for this. There is a sound, a bzzzz. It started off and got louder and louder and faster and faster.
DMT:The Spirit Molecule

The humming, buzzing noise seemed eerily similar to one that had disturbed him a few months earlier... His neighbor, yet another

CIA officer, had also heard odd noises, and to him they seemed 'mechanical-sounding'.

T. Moore|The Sydney Morning Herald

It all began with a whining, whirring sound.

DMT:The Spirit Molecule

"They are sensory organs, like the skin." To suggest that sound might enter the ear and thenceforth shock the brain is, says O'Sullivan, "an anatomical nonsense".

T. Moore|The Sydney Morning Herald

...when Joe Simonton was attracted outside by a peculiar noise similar to "knobby tires on a wet pavement"... Simonton, who could see several instrument panels, heard a slow whining sound, similar to the hum of a generator.

J. Vallee|Passport To Magonia

It started with a sound. It was high-pitched like a tightly taut wire.

DMT:The Spirit Molecule

It passed within twenty yards of him, and Styles was able to see through the thing and hear the low roaring or rushing noise it was making.

P. Devereux|Earth Lights

There are surprising and remarkable consistencies among volunteers' reports of contact with nonmaterial beings. Sound and vibration build until the scene almost explosively shifts to an "alien" realm.

R. Strassman|DMT:The Spirit Molecule

It appears at about that time of life when the organism is at its high watermark of efficiency, at the age of thirty to forty years.

R. M. Bucke|Cosmic Consciousness

...a twenty-seven-year-old banana-grower, George Pedley, was driving his tractor in the vicinity of a swamp called Horseshoe Lagoon when he suddenly heard a loud hissing noise.

It "sounded like air escaping from a tire," he said. Then, twenty-five yards in front of him, he saw a machine rising from the swamp.

J. Vallee|Passport To Magonia

...a gouslar, when not fighting, would take his goussle and recite to his comrades heroic poems...the goussle: an instrument which emits droning monotonous sounds...in olden times, in Serbia, this instrument was played by minstrels, thirty years of age or more;...

W. M. Petrovitch|Hero Tales and Legends of the Serbians

There was the same pulsating vibration... The buzzing and kaleidoscopic shifting was intense and went on for a long time.

DMT:The Spirit Molecule

The object rose from the ground with a deafening buzzing sound and disappeared into the sky.

C. and J. Lorenzen|Flying Saucer Occupants

There was a sound, like a hum that turned into a whoosh, and then I was blasted out of my body at such speed, with such force, as if it were the speed of light...

There are sounds: high-pitched singing...simply part of the background noise of blasting through the void of the universe... There is a great roaring sound.

DMT:The Spirit Molecule

The spooky and pernicious sound-related incidents tapped into a tradition of febrile paranoia.

T. Moore|The Sydney Morning Herald

...consciousness is disturbed by a bright light, humming sounds, strange bodily vibrations or paralysis...

DMT:The Spirit Molecule

...and was making a peculiar noise which sounded like it came out of a pipe. They described it as similar to the noise made by a kazoo.

C. and J. Lorenzen|Flying Saucer Occupants

The cause and its effects seemed to be something entirely new. Smith's conclusion —that the victims had suffered a brain trauma, but without the typically obvious physical damage— inspired talk of 'the immaculate concussion'.

T. Moore|The Sydney Morning Herald

May the sound of this bell penetrate deep into the cosmos. Even in the darkest spots, living beings are able to hear it clearly, so that all suffering in them cease, understanding comes to their heart, and they transcend the path of sorrow and death.

Thich Nhat Hanh

He said it created "a strange noise" in his ears.

P. Devereux|Earth Lights

He knew that he must quickly find something to lift the spirits of his men, and after much thought it suddenly came to him.

What he needed most was to fill their ears with the sound of a victory drum, a drum which would resound with more power and volume than anyone has ever before imagined possible. "With such a drum, I would bring fear to the enemy and hope to my own men," the Emperor thought to himself.

Chinese Myth

A strange hum accompanied the appearance of a disc... Although no one else saw the landed discs or their occupants, several in the area heard the humming sound.

C. and J. Lorenzen|Flying Saucer Occupants

Next morning Coyote asked Old Man to go to his fish trap early. "I think I heard a noise in the night that sounded like fish caught in a trap," he said.

Voices of the Wind

A low humming sound became audible...

J. Vallee|Passport To Magonia

Another boy said he heard a "throbbing sound", and still another said he heard a "hissing sound".

C. and J. Lorenzen|Flying Saucer Occupants

He was awoken in the early hours of the morning by a buzzing sound.

P. Devereux|Earth Lights

He was lighting a cigarette before starting the tractor when he heard a high-pitched whistling sound.

C. and J. Lorenzen|Flying Saucer Occupants

—//—

Seeker; Man himself is *the King*, of *the Jungle*; *the Steward* of *the Garden*; that, surely *the King* of animals shall, perceive *the Voice*, of, *any and all gods*, before his furry brethren have even detected, a single vibration with, their ancient, *animal-senses*. That, surely *the King*, godlike in his awareness of, *his own Self*, shall hear, clearly, *his own Thundering Voice*, prior to any and all Other; that, surely *the Voice of the King*, shall frighten any and all of, the yet fearful animals of this garden, still wandering *the Abyss* without a lamp, resisting the call to approach, *the Light*.

The object glowed and made a faint swishing sound.
C. and J. Lorenzen|Flying Saucer Occupants

As I was trampling through the bush my attention was attracted by a familiar sound, a sound for all the world like the working of an air pump on a locomotive. I went at once in the direction of the sound...
J. Vallee|Passport To Magonia

As he walked across a piece of open ground on the outskirts of the city, ...he heard a strange humming sound, then saw two cones of light...
C. and J. Lorenzen|Flying Saucer Occupants

John M. Barclay was intrigued when his dog barked furiously and a high-pitched noise was heard.
J. Vallee|Passport To Magonia

On the top the father was unable to see anything unusual but he did hear a strange noise. Trevor subsequently suffered unfortunate after-effects: the following day his speech became impaired; three weeks later his left eye became blind, then this changed to his right eye and became almost total before easing. He also underwent a personality change and up to 1978 at least was still undergoing psychiatric treatment.
P. Devereux|Earth Lights

At the same time that this god's voice was heard, the rest of the god's voices were humming in the background, a sort of buzzing noise with no particular melody which came from somewhere in the back of the inside or near-outside region of her head.

R. Haskell|Gods, Voices, and the Bicameral Mind

...it took off at high speed, making a hissing sound which resembled the "sound of steam coming out of a boiler".

C. and J. Lorenzen|Flying Saucer Occupants

...made noise similar to a vacuum cleaner...

J. Vallee|Passport To Magonia

I heard the sound of the ocean
It was headed our way
Followed by thunder
The roar and the rain

I. Bluestone|Will We Remain?

What's that noise... A-a tsunami?!

J. Ito|Remina

With a shrieking noise the air will be sucked in by each tube and the petals will shoot the air far into the outer air.

Vymaanika Shaastra

I could hear the sound of a steady hum.
                    R. Strassman|Inner Paths to Outer Space

...a sound something like that produced when a newspaper is crushed...
                    C. A. Wickland|Thirty Years Among the Dead

Embrace your, rhythmic, evolution.

Local people also described it as a giant bird covered with large scales producing a metallic noise.
                    J. Vallee|Passport To Magonia

Are we listening?
Hymns of offering.
                                        Collective Soul

Besos de Noche

Seeker; are you, *feeling?* Embrace your own Self; that you might for the first time, truly, —*feel ...and see; the Infamous sweet kiss.* Embrace your evolution, Seeker; for, *Life, touches firmly,* —all those that, resist not the Embrace.

> *At the same time, she felt that someone was kissing her cheeks, but so softly and gently that she might have thought it was only the finest cotton down touching her.*
> J. Vallee|Passport To Magonia

> *Effects on tactile and gravitational senses can be pronounced.*
> R. Strassman|Inner Paths to Outer Space

> *The reddish yellow light was coming out of the sky at an angle of sixty degrees.*
> J. Vallee|Passport To Magonia

> *Then the whole globe tipped back at a sharp angle and shot off into the sky at an angle of about thirty to forty-five degrees.*
> C. and J. Lorenzen|Flying Saucer Occupants

All of a sudden, I was bathed in this white light from above, it felt like anti-gravity energy that lifted me up and out of my bed, and through the roof... It felt good to be weightless and floating up...

R. Strassman|Inner Paths to Outer Space

It didn't go in a straight line...

It went at an ever-increasing angle of up, and the last point we saw, it had to have been going up into the sky at a forty-five degree angle...

J. Mack|Abduction

There was a rush of wind as it took off at about a 45-degree angle, whereupon it vanished quickly into the sky.

C. and J. Lorenzen|Flying Saucer Occupants

...he looked out of the window and saw a semi-circle of white lights about three inches in diameter going down at an angle of 45 degrees into the trees.

J. Vallee|Passport To Magonia

It rose rapidly and silently into the sky at about a 45-degree angle toward the northeast...

C. and J. Lorenzen|Flying Saucer Occupants

The table was tilted to a forty-five degree angle as one of the beings began to issue commands to another.

J. Mack|Abduction

...it took off, flying into the west at an angle of 45 degrees.

C. and J. Lorenzen|Flying Saucer Occupants

...when they noticed a brightly lighted object ahead of their car at an angle of elevation of approximately 45 degrees.

J. Vallee|Passport To Magonia

The angle was an obtuse angle, and I remember thinking as I woke that had he made it a right or acute angle, I should have both suffered and "seen" still more, and should probably have died.

W. James|The Varieties of Religious Experience

Then the object took off at a 45-degree angle and was gone in just a few seconds.

C. and J. Lorenzen|Flying Saucer Occupants

Finally I felt myself tumbling gently and sliding backward away from this Light, sliding down a ramp.

DMT:The Spirit Molecule

She described a metal ramp, angled at forty-five degrees...
                                                    J. Mack|Abduction

I feel a tingling in my body. A strange lifting sensation.
                                                    DMT:The Spirit Molecule

Based on the location and climate of the place, some solar panels are installed at an angle of 45 degrees for optimal solar energy production.
                                                    Wikipedia|45-Degree Angle

The 45th parallel north is often called the halfway point between the equator and the North Pole...
                                                    Wikipedia|45th Parellel

Number 45 possess great spiritual energy. People with this Angel Number are often full of great ideas. This number also reflects their incredibly strong intuition.
                                                    Angel Number 45

The number 45 gives innovation, the ability to research deeply and communicate. The digits in the number 45 have the digit sum 9 which resonates with the planet Mars. 45 is often written as 45/9 where the digit sum is placed after the slash. To understand 45 more in depth we recommend you also read more about the digit sum 9...
                                                    Numerology Number 45

Number 9 meaning in numerology represents the great mental and spiritual realizations, it is the number of the initiation, because it marks the end of a phase of spiritual development and the beginning of another higher stage...

Numerology Number 9

...private pilot Kenneth Arnold claimed that he saw a string of nine, shiny unidentified flying objects flying past Mount Rainier...

Wikipedia|Kenneth Arnold UFO Sighting

THE SIGNS

Nor have they any correct notion of the control which God exercises over the affairs of the world. The prevailing notion seems to be that God, after having made the world and filled it with inhabitants, retired to some remote corner of the universe and has allowed the affairs of the world to come under the control of evil spirits; and hence the only religious worship that is ever performed is directed to these spirits, the object of which is to court their favor, or ward off the evil effects of their displeasure.

R. H. Nassu|Fetichism

SEEKER; [*MIGHTY-FLAME-THROWER*]; THE ANCIENTS proclaim, *sadly,* *"our gods have left us"*; the gods proclaim, *assuredly, "we shall return"*; while the Modern Man proclaims, *unknowingly, "I am, the return; I am, the accumulation of all before me; I am, the evolution"*.

The gods of the ancients have kept their promise. They have returned. But they do not come to us from across the chasm of interstellar space. They come somehow from within us.

J. Keel|The Cosmic Question

"Why do you not worship him?" Promptly they reply: "Yes, he made us; but, having made us, he abandoned us, does not care for us; he is far from us. Why should we care for him? He does not help

nor harm us. It is the spirits who can harm us whom we fear and worship, and for whom we care."
                                                    R. H. Nassau|Fetichism

Realize; that, *the Return* is, *The Sign; message; a change; evolution.* That, the gods have always been *premonitory;* that, the revelation of *the Story of Man,* shall be *the Truth that, —unites us in liberation.*

...private pilot Kenneth Arnold claimed that he saw a string of nine, shiny unidentified flying objects flying past Mount Rainier... The encounter gave him an "eerie feeling"...
                                    Wikipedia|Kenneth Arnold UFO Sighting

We have to prepare ourselves to view the actual mechanisms of ESP quite independent of the old labels...
                                                                    I. Swann

...think, differently...

Two forest observers were in a canyon... when they saw a disk-shaped flying object...
                                            J. Vallee|Passport to Magonia

At the time, these signs were novelties. But I noticed how much information was really contained in them, without the use of words.
                                                                    I. Swann

Seeker; you are, not what you think you are; you are, so much more; that, *the Sign is the Sign;* that, *the Sign is the Reflection of, your very own signature;* that, *the Signs are the Signs* that, you, are more than you have *thought and been taught.*

On December 10, 1946, six Curtis Commando R5C transport planes carrying more than 200 U.S. Marines leave San Diego en route to Seattle. The aircraft, flying entirely by instruments at an altitude of 9,000 feet, encounter heavy weather over southwestern Washington. Four turn back, landing at the Portland Airport; one manages to land safely in Seattle, but the sixth plane, carrying 32 Marines, vanishes.

D. C. McClary|History Link

On June 24, 1947, Arnold was flying from Chehalis, Washington, in a CallAir A-2 on a business trip.

Wikipedia|Kenneth Arnold UFO Sighting

Under great emergencies they looked beyond the lower beings, and asked help of that Superior before doing so, they prayed to him, imploring him as Father to help;...

R. H. Nassau|Spiritual Fetichism

Seeker; the wise Man considers, *the Family-Man*; the wise Man considers, *the Man* on, business; *business-minded*, in the moment; *a hunter, a provider*; seeking, a way to provide for his, family. The wise Man knows, *the Family*, is *the Man*; the wise Man considers the pressure upon, *the Family-Man*, to provide; *stress, seeking of guidance.* The wise Man considers the benefits of, *a large kill*; a significant harvest; a hidden treasure, found; *the Lottery-Ticket; —a year of income, in just one afternoon.*

The wise Man knows, *the Family-Man especially seeks, a way, a path, toward liberation*; freedom; from job; from stress; from loneliness; from, *all*. The wise Man knows, regardless of the reason, on June 24, 1947, there was a Man, *seeking; —something!* The wise Man knows, when *the Man humbly and sincerely seeks, the Cosmos which he is, —has always answered.*

The 32 U.S. Marines remain entombed forever on Mount Rainier. In 1946, it was the worst accident, in numbers killed aboard an aircraft, in United States aviation history... At dawn on Wednesday, December 11, 1946, Army, Navy, and Coast Guard search planes were poised to start an intensive search of the area where the aircraft was presumed to have disappeared... The search for the missing plane resumed the next summer, after some of the snow had melted... Families of the missing men offered a $5,000 reward to anyone finding the plane.

D. C. McClary|History Link

Understand; the wise Man hears a call from *the Collective*, to seek and find, *parts of its own Self*; the wise Man perceives the desperation and prayers of, *the Love*, seeking, the souls lost amidst the snow.

He made a brief detour after learning of a $5,000 reward (equivalent to $61,000 today) for the discovery of a U.S. Marine Corps C-46 transport airplane that had crashed near Mount Rainier. ...he gave up his search and started heading eastward... He saw a bright flashing light, similar to sunlight reflecting from a mirror. The reflections came from flying objects...

Wikipedia|Kenneth Arnold UFO Sighting

Realize; the wise Man knows, it is at the moment of, *breaking; giving-in; giving-up; surrendering of control*; the wise Man knows, it is the greatest moment of stress, and desperation, that Man begins to truly see.

The rider who had heard the voices said, "Yesterday they all spoke, but now they have changed their forms." Suddenly they saw Rainbow who came in the form of a wheel. He asked, "What are you looking for?" "We are searching for our lost people," said the people.

A. Metraux

"I noticed to the left of me a chain which looked to me like the tail of a Chinese kite, kind of weaving... they seemed to flip and flash in the sun, just like a mirror... they seemed to kind of weave in and out right above the mountaintops..."

Wikipedia|Kenneth Arnold UFO Sighting

Seeker; the wise Man perceives, what, perhaps, is not at first obvious; for *the Light,* can indeed be blinding; that, the flipping and flashing *of* light, in a mirror, is *meant* to grab the attention; *you.* That, *a message awaits, he who sees, the Flashes;* that, lost adventurers nearing *the Peak,* of a great mountain, seeking help, shall surely attempt to capture *the Gaze* of, *the Aviator above, by reflecting a bright Light;* the more brilliant, the better; that, every child knows to *follow the Light* of, *the Rainbow;* for treasure shall surely be found!

It glowed with a bluish-green light, made a whistling sound, rose... then left at fantastic speed. A strange metal block is said to have been found at the spot.

J. Vallee|Passport to Magonia

Understand; *the debris is never left-behind nor deposited by, the Light; the Light,* merely attracts your attention to *what had already been; the Light, is, simply, awareness.*

There were a lot of elves... maybe four of them appeared at the side of a stretch of interstate highway I travel regularly. They commanded the scene, it was their terrain!

They were about my height. They held up placards, showing me these incredibly beautiful, complex, swirling geometric scenes in them... They wanted me to look!

R. Strassman|DMT:The Spirit Molecule

According to a report, Bigelow's company had 46 scientists studying the materials and analyzing military data on the phenomenon. "Rapid response teams" were also formed and dispatched to scenes of UFO events to collect material and data...
Gaia

In a group of buildings in Las Vegas, the government stockpiles alloys and other materials believed to be associated with UFOs.
R. Letzter|Scientific American

...the blue morpho doesn't use pigment in their wings. Instead, they rely on a unique type of natural metamaterial that gives their wings an iridescent blue colour...Just like the blue morpho, the human eye can exhibit a natural form of metamaterial that reflects blue but selectively absorbs other colours.
META

Realize; the military Man responds to threats in *the Sky,* and presumes to, *believe, have a belief, faith, that, the Enemy left his trash behind.*

The wise Man hears *threat* and, giggles; the wise Man is fearless; the wise Man recalls, *he has no enemies;* the wise Man fears not the ubiquitous *UAP, UFO, nor dancing fairy-light;* the wise Man understands *the Message;* the wise Man grasps *the UFO, as, the ESP; hear and see!*

The wise Man, seeks treasure at the end of, *every flashing rainbow-of-lights.* That, the fiercest military the World has yet known, shall shoot at and hide from, its own shimmery shadow, while the truly wise Man shall, *sprint toward his!*

Like snowfall, smoke, sun, wind, fire, firefly, lightning, crystal, moon, these forms, coming before, gradually manifest the Brahman in Yoga.

Swami Vivekananda|Raja Yoga

...we can engineer systems that can interact with and manipulate light in entirely new ways. It's kind of neat to see an example in the case of a metal like gold. We usually think of gold as a bulk material that is reflective, yellowish and shiny. Even when you go down to the nanoscale, gold is still gold. But by specifying the geometry of nanoscale gold, we can change the color of gold from yellow to green or red, and it can support many other types of optical properties that we don't associate with bulk gold.

J. Fan|Stanford Nanofabrication Facility

...we can understand that any impedance we may encounter, which degrades the clarity of the psychic information, comes from erroneous conscious misinterpretations of the psychic information, the misinterpretation being automatically superimposed over the true information.

I. Swann

Two prospectors are said to have observed a dish-shaped object land.

J. Vallee|Passport to Magonia

It was only after I learned to detach myself from the power of these labels that some of ESP's mechanisms revealed themselves.

I. Swann

A hunter, who had lost his way in the mountains, observed approaching lights that seemed to land.

J. Vallee|Passport to Magonia

I'm asking questions and getting answers.

R. Strassman|DMT:The Spirit Molecule

They immersed a hose in the lake, then took off. Fisherman later reported a green moss forming on the lake.

J. Vallee|Passport to Magonia

The wise Man understands *the Message;* the wise Man appreciates the warning to, *not drink the water.*

Hearing a commotion in his barn, a farmer observed an object... light gray in color and lit up inside. It resembled a half egg... Numerous livestock died 'mysteriously' in the area after the sighting.

J. Vallee|Passport to Magonia

When asked to clarify his statement on the interaction of UAPs and nuclear energy, Elizondo said, 'UAPs have an active interest in our nuclear technology...'

D. Phenix|Mystery Wire

Realize, Seeker; the tired government man-of-deception shall, in his fearfulness, fearlessly lead *the Fearful;* the wise Man shall see *the UAP* as, the messenger it surely is and has always been from *the Dawn;* the wise Man knows: —*don't shoot the Messenger.*

The world's most important powers—the Soviet Union, the United States, and the People's Republic of China—have mounted increasingly large programs to research extrasensory potentials...It is worth noting that modern Russian scientists have coined a term that incorporates all these facets quite well—they use the term 'extrasensory perception' only rarely. Their term is "bioinformation". This has the advantage of cutting beneath all the arbitrary labels Westerners habitually use to describe phenomena such as clairvoyance, precognition, telepathy, and ESP. ...The use of bioinformation has one truly great advantage. It focuses the individual's attention on getting "information" rather than upon some hypothetical faculty that might be implied by ESP.

Ingo Swann

Speaking to a reporter for the Associated Press, Arnold said: "This whole thing has gotten out of hand. I want to talk to the FBI or someone. Half the people look at me as a combination of Einstein, Flash Gordon and screwball. I wonder what my wife back in Idaho thinks." A sighting by a United Airlines crew of another nine disk-like objects over Idaho on July 4 probably garnered more newspaper coverage than Arnold's original sighting...

Wikipedia|Kenneth Arnold UFO Sighting

On the evening of July 4th at Boise, Idaho, Captain Smith was walking up the ramp to board his plane, flight 105, for a trip to Seattle when someone mentioned the massive wave of saucers taking place all day over the northwest. Captain Smith joked: "I'll believe in those disks when I see them."

Project 1947

He who has given up all attachment, all fear, and all anger, he whose whole soul has gone unto the Lord, he who has taken refuge in the Lord, whose heart has become purified, with whatsoever desire he comes to the Lord, He will grant that to him. Therefore worship Him through knowledge, love, or renunciation.

Swami Vivekananda|Raja Yoga

ENTRY

*00/00/1967|1600UTC *MALMSTRM|AFB|MONTANA*
M.A.S.E.|ANTARCTC'SRVR;_AF.OSI-FLDRCRDR07-16BIT
M.A.S.E./ERR;...MLTPLVRSNDTCTD;..INTERCEPT ;...
BGIN-TXMSSN; DGTLCNVRSTN;...

... ...

AF-OSI|AGNTI94:
>>_____?;\\//||;ERR[DTAUNSYNC;];
  "So... you saw the security-tapes?"

                    AF-OSI|SNRAGNT-IC:
          >>_____?;\\//||;ERR[DTAUNSYNC;];
                                    "Oh yeah."

  AF-OSI|AGNTI94:
>>_____?;\\//||;ERR[DTAUNSYNC;];
  "All three tapes?"

                    AF-OSI|SNRAGNT-IC:
          >>_____?;\\//||;ERR[DTAUNSYNC;];
                              "Fuckin'-A I did."

  AF-OSI|AGNTI94:
>>_____?;\\//||;ERR[DTAUNSYNC;];
  "And...? Your thoughts?"

AF-OSI|SNRAGNT-IC:

>>_____?;\\//\|;ERR[DTAUNSYNC;];

"Well, it's pretty damn obvious don't you think? Same as all the others. This fucker says it's a UFO attack, or sees a fireball somehow, and all of a sudden the switches and dials are all flipped and screwy. And yet, each and every goddamned time, we catch the fuckers falling asleep on duty, on multiple cameras, half-waking-up in some sort of unconscious Roman Catholic styled devil-possessed state, frantically smashing the control panel and wetting themselves as tears stream down their expressionless faces, mouths agape like a damn Egyptian pharaoh."

AF-OSI|AGNTI94:

>>_____?;\\//\|;ERR[DTAUNSYNC;];

"So, better call those CPMI guys again huh?"

AF-OSI|SNRAGNT-IC:

>>_____?;\\//\|;ERR[DTAUNSYNC;];

"They're already here."

..INTERCEPT;STOP-TXMSSN; DGTLCNVRSTN;...

The End, Seeker, is always *The Beginning*.